NEW DIRECTIONS 46

In memoriam
TENNESSEE WILLIAMS
1911–1983

N D
New Directions in Prose and Poetry 46

Edited by J. Laughlin
with Peter Glassgold and Frederick R. Martin

A New Directions Book

Copyright © 1983 by New Directions Publishing Corporation
Library of Congress Catalog Card Number: 37-1751

All rights reserved. Except for brief passages quoted in a newspaper, magazine, radio, or television review, no part of this book may be reproduced in any form or by any means, electronic or mechanical, including photocopying and recording, or by any information storage and retrieval system, without permission in writing from the Publisher.

ACKNOWLEDGMENTS

Grateful acknowledgment is made to the editors and publishers of books and magazines in which some of the material in this volume first appeared: for Deirdra Baldwin, Contraband, Spectrum, Three Sisters (Copyright © 1981 by Deirdra Baldwin); for Maclin Bocock, Fiction (Copyright © 1982 by Maclin Bocock); for Doug Crowell, Crazyhorse (Copyright © 1980 by Crazyhorse, The University of Arkansas at Little Rock); for Jorge Edwards, Fiction (Copyright © 1978 by Fiction, Inc.); for Russell Haley, Islands (New Zealand); for Mary Jane White, Crazyhorse, The Anthology of American Poetry and Magazine Verse (Monitor Book Company, Inc.), The Iowa Review (Copyright © 1982 by Mary Jane White).

Philippe Denis' "Ten Poems," as translated by Mark Irwin, are included in Notebook of Shadows: Selected Poems 1974–1980 (Copyright © 1982 by Mark Irwin), published by The Globe Press in 1982. The original French texts are from Cahiers d'ombres (© Mercure de France, 1974) and Revif (© Maeght, 1978).

The following poems are quoted in full, and also appear in Old English translation by Peter Glassgold, in Hwæt!: "Illustrious Ancestors," by Denise Levertov, from Collected Earlier Poems 1940–1960 (Copyright © 1958 by Denise Levertov); "Boy's Room," by George Oppen, from Collected Poems (Copyright © 1965 by George Oppen); "Delia Rexroth," by Kenneth Rexroth, from Collected Shorter Poems (Copyright 1949 by Kenneth Rexroth); "By Frazier Creek Falls," by Gary Snyder, from Turtle Island (Copyright © 1974 by Gary Snyder). All are reprinted and translated by permission of New Directions. "It Does Me Good," by James Laughlin, from In Another Country (Copyright © 1959 by New Directions; Copyright © 1978 by James Laughlin) is reprinted and translated by permission of City Lights Books.

The original Portuguese text of "Plaza Mauá," by Clarice Lispector, from A Via Crucis do Corpo, © Heirs of Clarice Lispector

Manufactured in the United States of America
First published clothbound (ISBN: 0-8112-0865-6) and as New Directions Paperbook 553 (ISBN: 0-8112-0866-4) in 1983
Published simultaneously in Canada by George J. McLeod, Ltd., Toronto

New Directions Books are published for James Laughlin
by New Directions Publishing Corporation,
80 Eighth Avenue, New York 10011

CONTENTS

Dierdra Baldwin
    Five Poems   63

Carol Jane Bangs
    Neakhanie, '82   54

Maclin Bocock
    La Humanidad   125

Nicholas Born
    Seven Poems   174

Ernesto Cardenal
    Two Poems   105

Doug Crowell
    Work   24

Pablo Antonio Cuadra
    Two Poems   130

Philippe Denis
    Ten Poems   142

Joseph Donahue
    Five Poems   68

Jorge Edwards
    Experience   147

Peter Glassgold, ed. and trans.
    Hwæt! Five American Modernist Poets in Old English
    Translation   36

J. B. Goodenough
    Eight Poems   48

Lars Gustafsson
    Three Poems   18

Russell Haley
    The Cosmetic Factory   110

William Holinger
    A Young Woman's Winter Night   44

André Lefevere
    A Yellow Rabbit Full of Helium   179

Denise Levertov
    The Gardener   60

Clarice Lispector
    Plaza Mauá   74

Michael McGuire
    The Snow Tunnel   138

Ursule Molinaro
    Dr. Arnold Biedermeier's Suicide Parlors   98

Robert Nichols
    Clara Remembered   3

Alistair Paterson, ed.
    Seven New Zealand Poets   78

A. Poulin, Jr.
    Begin Again   159

Aleksis Rannit
    Two Poems   119

Geoffrey Rips
    La Vita Nuova   171

Mary Jane White
    Five Poems   165

Tennessee Williams
    The Color of a House   1

Notes on Contributors   182

THE COLOR OF A HOUSE

TENNESSEE WILLIAMS

In some village, tucked away among ravines of rolling green
    country,
        cool and mistily pastoral
        with warnings of deer crossing,
            luminous squares of metal at night with profiles, black
                against orange,
leaping as if performing the last leap of a foredoomed prey,
    I hope that you will not disregard the advice
to paint your house no odd and conspicuous color, or contrast of
    colors,
especially if the house is rectangular with a low-peaked roof.
To do so would be to invite misfortune too early, a guest which,
in any event involving the destinies of house builders
does not wait upon invitation. The low-peaked roof
would provide small space for an attic to house the lunatic one
who drifts apart till requiring separate enclosure:
screaming ecstatically in its fantasies of that which is its
    reality,
so alien to your own.
        This imposes a most unwanted distinction upon the house
and inhabitants of it.
            The ones sufficiently past infancy to enquire, "What is it,
            the cry?"

can be given what answer, intelligible to their beginning-to-be
  formed minds?
And so they turn strange as well, their faces pale, even their
  eyes appearing
to turn a lighter color through disturbed speculations.
    Abruptly a cry is taken up by a cry. It springs from one
      to another,
and the house, oddly painted, is more and more unfavorably
  distinguished
from other houses.
    Do what, then? Paint the house the least conspicuous color,
mottle it with variant greens such as those of the country?
    This action would be no longer effective, I warn you:
not lost in the mistily variant green of the country.
Finally any color that you apply to the house will fail to prevent
  its being not only set
apart but afire. And your outcries of fire will not bring to
  the house
those living near it and too long fearful of it.

              . . .

    From the top of a silo in rolling green country
I have seen large birds of a blue-black luster sweep suddenly
  skyward.
I looked back. They were gone. That quickly!

    Comfort me, Love, for in these words you must know that
      I have confessed to you
fear of a madness whose only escape is to death.

CLARA REMEMBERED

ROBERT NICHOLS

1

In the late summer the surface of the lake smoothed, the sky quickened and deepened. There was a day set aside to pick blueberries. The hill where the blueberry farm was was at the end of the Grafton line. Everyone took pails. And these had to be filled. It was a serious business. She was about five then. My uncle Sylvio said to her:
—You play and I'll fill your pail.
—Won't mamma see?
—Ne t'inquiets pa'. Don't worry.
So all day she played hidden from her mother under the bronzing leaves and deep umbels of the high-bush blueberries. Till the rare holiday ended and they paid the man his fee and the whole family went home by trolley.

. .

And years later she said to her husband (this was in a room outside the army compound at Camp Devens Mass).
—Give me a child.
—I don't want a child. Who am I and what have I been in this world that I should want to reproduce myself?
—I want you. I love you. They're sending you away somewhere.

They'll send you overseas and you may be killed.
—Yes. But how can I be certain of it?

The first of their many mistakes?

NOVEMBER 11 1918   ARMISTICE IS SIGNED   GENERAL PERSHING CONTINUES TO HOLD FORCES IN READINESS ALONG THE FRONT LINES   SPOKESMAN SAYS A.E.F. TO BE DEMOBILIZED SOMETIME BEFORE CHRISTMAS . . .   CONTINUED FIGHTING REPORTED IN THE ARDENNES SECTOR . . .

In this way I was born. And this is the way I was told to remember it. Can I help that?

. .

My mother's name was Clara
    a name she disliked
the harsh summons of grandmother calling it:
        "Clara"
and changed it to Claire
        Claire Lalone
In order the Lalone children: Corinne
    Ernest   Sylvio   my mother Clara
      Anita   Roland   and the two babies of the family
(a late blessing for Mamma)
        Jeanne and Marcel
Why do these names
    for me
      have such sweetness?

2

We were throwing snowballs. Furious fights in the schoolyard (Saint Joseph's) as the nuns stood and looked out the window. The girls screaming (among them is Clara) also scraping up snow with a mitten to throw at each other. But tenderly
    as if to say: Here. Here is the first snow
        fallen today.

Snow lay in heaps on the tops of picket fences along
Fairmont Avenue as we came home from school.
RAT TAT TAT   we went along knocking it off with our stick
HELLO WORCESTER MASSACHUSETTS WE'RE
TWELVE YEARS OLD   YOU CAN'T STOP US!
We salute you grimy houses where the householders are all inside   scrubbing linoleum. They are out to church praying. They have left their furnaces working for them in the basements. Snow has drifted against the baseboards and up under the demure skirts of houses insulated with tar paper.

And on the sidewalks bruised by the chutes there are lumps and brilliants of coal littering the dry snow.

On the way to Heard's candystore we found a bird frozen by the curbstone   which we recognized from the summer. It was our tree-boarder   the one who had stolen our cherries.
        Pray for the little bird
        all you furnaces.

· ·

The house was one of those two-story wood structures built around the 1900s on what was beginning to be called "French Hill" for the Canadian immigrant families settling in to work in the steel and textile mills. Later there would be those ugly tenements covering the hills farther out painted in browns and greens with the three outside porches stacked one above the other hung with damp wash. But this one was something to be proud of! It was better than the rest by dint of hard work. On March days my mother and her sisters would sit in the front parlor in stiff dresses looking out between the lace curtains. What would go by? Well, the milk wagon for one thing. Behind them they felt the weight of the house   the parlor in its dry weeds   the yellowing photographs of baptisms on the piano   the saints calendar given them by Fr. Thibbedeau   the heavy mahogany bookcase which was never opened except in winter to take out overshoes. And behind that the "dining room" where Mamma worked   where she kept her sewing machine and which was always piled with strips of fur and coat trimmings lying over the chairs and sofa. And behind that the kitchen where the scrubbed linoleum began.

And beside the porch the cherry tree   with its limbs and leaves. And its black ripe cherries! Protect them, Mamma, from thieves!

And upstairs room after room (Or so it seemed to them. Actually it was small and would be made over into an apartment for Sylvio) of beds to be made by the girls. Early morning it was like a boarding-house   the heaviness and limpness of blankets being aired   half-visible secrets and bureau drawers   the quilts spilled on the floor and mattresses which still seemed heavy and leaden with sleepers.

And around five Pappa would come from the machine shop and all the boys who were working (except for Marcel)   that was Sylvio Roland Ernest   all back from one job or another after school. It would be impossible then for Mamma to sit on top of everything   as if by brute force   as if silencing the heart. And the guard of the house would be down   the grim weight lightened   and the air boisterous with shouts and jokes.

. .

Her lover at that time was duB. H., a well-known literary figure. (In Charleston, South Carolina 1940. She had gone there after separating from my father.) DuB. H. was a charmer but also a man of genuine perceptions, and he was taken with her. He stroked her hair. It was beginning to gray but she still had her figure   which elicited him deeply. He floated a tangerine blossom toward her across the table polished with glints. He began by rubbing the tips of her ears   then her scalp with his extremely delicate fingers almost like another woman's. And so down the filaments of her long hair. He massaged her throat   and whispered   in her ear:

—Forget him. I don't want you to think about him anymore.

(and again softly and gently)

—I understand everything.

As he touched her she felt her throat stiffen. It wasn't that she didn't wish to respond to him. But at those moments she became cold as a stone   as if locked up inside. The pivots of her body were like granite. Making love would be quite hopeless.

. .

Thought
       like a small bird
flickers out suddenly into the open
    & asks to be seen
And quickly. See the wing marks!
the thin flight of vermillion between points

Out of the dark shadow within the tree
            thought
    makes itself visible
        & sings its song
words like: —I understand that/I want you
                    to believe that . . .

Thought ruffles its feathers & sings:
    —Breathe easily / Don't be afraid of him
YOU CAN BEGIN AGAIN   NEW

Thought   flickers its birdwings
    or flexes itself
little green firesnake looping over the wax leaves

3 THE MERCER TOURING CAR ROMANCE & OTHER REMI-
NISCENCES

It was June the time when the floribunda climbers under the side porch were in their first full bloom   the month of brides. Corinne had taken her sister aside   she was saying:
    —Why don't you do it? We'll have wild fun!
    —All the way to Montreal? Clara wondered. In his car?
    —He's such a dreamy man. And such a gentleman. Corinne signed.
    Corinne: the eldest and wisest of the four sisters. She was always ready with advice.
    —I'll handle Mamma.
    —Don't you dare mention it! Just the thought of it made Clara's blood run cold. It was Mamma's job to punish—and that meant

sticks, shoes, hairbrushes. She pulled Clara's hair and shook her if she was bad until her teeth rattled. But Pappa was not such a strict Catholic. My God! the idea of having a Protestant boyfriend who was not from French Hill. But now Clara was almost as strong as Mamma.

The sun flooded in among the starchy curtains. It picked out pieces of silk and trimmings on the run under Mamma's worktable. A waltz was playing over the Atwater Kent radio. Also a new telephone had been installed several days earlier, with a ring-box of polished wood. —Ding-a-ling-a-ling   this telephone now rang.

It was Charles!

—He wants to speak to you, Corinne. And Clara moved away from the instrument as far as she could (looking fierce) to the other side of the room. But she could hear the voice at the other end of the receiver singing

"Tell me miss
　　is this the right switch
　　　　to Ipswich . . . "

while Corinne giggled. Corinne pressed the mouthpiece between her fat breasts. Poor ugly Corinne. She kept shrieking and agreeing with Charles, then glancing Clara's way. The conversation lasted for twenty minutes.

—He's absolutely mad for you, her sister announced. He can't stand it.

—Well, I've decided something. I'm not going to see him again. Never. It's not worth all the trouble.

—You're a little nitwit, Corinne told her. You'll be sorry, what girl gets a chance like this?

But the next week they were speeding toward Montreal, Clara and Corinne in the back seat of Charles's red-and-black leather upholstered Mercer, Charles and Hurtle the chauffeur up front. Charles had given Corinne his promise to behave. Every once in a while Hurtle gave him a chance to drive. This he did with great style, leaning over the dashboard and peering into the wind under his tweed cap. He was a real racer. The Mercer was a fast car on the level but going uphill it didn't have the pull. The passengers, that is Charles,

Corinne, and Clara, had to get out and walk beside it carrying their suitcases, while Hurtle remained at the wheel.

They had never been in the real country before, except for the blueberry holidays. A holiday!

After dinner they went to find the ballroom at the resort hotel. They found it empty. Corinne played the piano. She knew the songs from *Emilia* and *The Red Mill* and *The Desert Song*, while Charles and Clara waltzed. But in the middle of a slow one he grabbed her and began kissing her passionately on the neck . . . and Clara socked him. Then she burst into tears. Corinne comforted her. She took her by the shoulders still sobbing and led her back through the hotel to their room down what seemed to be miles and miles of burgundy-colored carpeted corridors. Charles left the hotel and took the train back to Worcester.

The next morning they were awakened by the bellboy with a formal note of apology from Charles. He accused himself of deep guilt. He had broken his gentleman's word—it had been the basis of the whole agreement with Corinne, of her coming with her kid sister. So he had gone, not to embarrass them further. But shouldn't they continue on to Montreal as planned? He was leaving them the Mercer car and Hurtle to be at their disposal.

And flowers! When they opened the large boxes the emerald wrapping paper was still humid and beaded with dew. The rich fragrance of flowers filled the room. He had bought out the whole greenhouse, and sent them dozens and dozens of tall-stemmed American Beauty roses!

That summer the girls stayed in Montreal with their Aunt's "Canuck" family, the Flammants. They lived in a district to the south of the city behind the dockyards. Even after they had been staying there several months the girls couldn't be sure how the Flammants lived, and did not approve anyway. Their Aunt Therese had wild frizzy hair, a coarse laugh, and deep circles under her eyes which made her look as though she'd been beaten up. There was a daughter called Carmen. Therese's husband was unemployed and was drunk most of the time on port wine. They found they had to do most of the work. That summer was unbearably hot in the Montreal slums.

They went to a few movies in the neighborhood but otherwise didn't see much of the city. They didn't like any of Carmen's friends.

Toward the end of August they received a letter from Charles begging to be allowed to come. The summer was about over anyway   and they soon would have to be going home to Mamma. She hadn't been thinking about him much really   but when he did arrive Clara was relieved. How she had missed him! She had never in her whole life known anyone so considerate and attractive. She realized that she was deeply in love with him.

. .

In a way   they retraced old steps . . .
    my grandfather's family had migrated
from Canada around the middle of the last century
        and settled in upstate New York

Lavenus had grown up doing farming
    then had become a journeyman
        installing box-making machinery
On a job in Worcester Mass.   he had met Rose

age 18   the fragrant Rose
    my own grandmother
whose name belied her temper
    fell in love with her

She had come down directly from Montreal
    & still tied to the family
probably went back & forth quite a bit but
    still had the gumption to strike on her own

dressmaking. A family connection would have told her
    about opportunities in Worcester.
        There
    met & married Lavenus

We are speaking of the scope & details
                of migrations
        . . . *by sea from Brittany*
Grandmother born in Three Rivers Canada
     remembers
           a small child sitting on top of the palisades
& seeing wolves

4

For the children on Fairmont Avenue their territory was the street, the sidewalk. Steep driveways going down to the garage—at the bottom the Lalone boys shot marbles. Even the back porch . . . Immediately "free" of the house Clara rushes down the front steps pulling on her coat and "out the door." Her eyes are for the outside world . . . also rushing to meet her. A neighbor's greeting. A girlfriend is holding her schoolbooks for her by the strap. She stands on one foot her hair cascading down, bending down to straighten her lisle stocking. Once they were playing hopscotch on the street shouting, Clara's eyes alight. Her mother came out of the house and grabbed her by the hair. She shook her till her teeth rattled, screaming that she was wearing out her shoes.

  . . . Stories of early Worcester Mass. family poverty
        For each child (there were 8) two pair of shoes
     one for school
           the other for church service or parties.
        The worry of buying shoes probably a pressure
     on grandmother
during the blueberrying expeditions.

—Where were you gone so long? asked Mamma of Clara and Roland (this is another story).

—Mamma (pleadingly): We weren't gone so long, we had to come all the way back from City Hall.

The trolley was marked CITY HALL. About that time Roland would have been around eight and Clara ten. Mamma had sent them to the town center on some errand. It was a mile and a half way at the bottom French Hill. She had given them a dime each for carfare. They had walked the whole way back, to spend it on candy. All-day suckers probably.

The sisters had many jobs, among them my mother worked in a candystore when she was thirteen. Later she worked at Sherer's Department store in downtown Worcester. (And next to Woolworth's where I used to go myself when I was six and spend afternoons lost with the lead soldiers in the upstairs toy department, Scotch Highlanders mostly.) My mother bragged that she was the first woman soda jerker in the State of Massachusetts, at Sherer's. It could have been. She would have gotten on quickly because of her "spark." There was a gay recklessness about her and her large eyes would have challenged the manager. Try me. She had started in Sherer's in the thread and needle department and stole money by keeping some pennies aside and ringing up the wrong amount on the cash register.

The Lalone girls all having the same problem where they worked (all save Carinne) of being too personable and good-looking. One by one they would come back from a job in distress. Rose looking up from her sewing machine:
 —Why are you back home? So soon?
 —Oh, Mamma, I had to.
 —Ques qu'ces' passé? You can tell Mamma, dear.
 Tears. The treachery of the storekeeper. —Oh Mamma it was awful. I was behind the counter, he grabbed me and tried to kiss me. So I left.
 —Naturally. Tomorrow you must look for another job. Mamma's eyes rolled up to heaven to call God to witness. Stuck in the mirror a strand of palm from Palm Sunday . . . Her tone would soften, she might even put her arm around them. That they had tried and been victimized
  for their beauty . . .
was one of the few feelings she shared with them.

5

On Sundays in those days my mother took me, an only child growing up on Cedar Street, over to the house on Fairmont Avenue for spaghetti dinner. The journey was by trolley down from Elm Park past the old railroad station and through the underpass—later my father and I would wait here for certain trains—and out onto Commercial Street and the Jewish section, and up to French Hill. The trolley passed Saint Joseph's church and school. On these Sundays at my grandmother's I would have been struck by the sheer excitement of so many people jammed into a small house and of feelings unrestrained—after the sad emptiness of my own large home. I can see the sisters gathering about Clara. Their arms thrown about me. —But Clara, he has your eyes . . . Yes, *French* eyes . . . like a Lalone! They embrace me. (I am five years old.) We all crowd into the kitchen to eat spaghetti with grandmother's sauce with green peppers made the night before. Some of the Lalone men are married now. Ernest with a boy about my own age. There was Marcel, Clara's brother, my own uncle but only two years older than me. I invited Marcel to my house to play with my electric trains.

Wine . . . ribald jokes. Sylvio comes out of the toilet next to the kitchen (you can hear flushing). —What was he doing in there so long? The women laugh. My grandmother Rose smiles distantly, as if she didn't know English.

. .

My grandfather, that is my father's father, had an "electric," an automobile in which he used to pay his doctor's calls. This was in what was called the "Elm Park section." I remember once driving in it, my mother and I in the back seat with a lap robe and a speaking tube, and Hurtle and the cook in the front seat, we were going shopping . . . In the attic I had a playroom with the electric trains—unimaginably expensive. I remember too standing at the window. This is in the Irish maid's room. She is pointing in the sky. We are watching Lindbergh fly back (from Boston) after his trip over the Atlantic. Or do I imagine this?

. .

My other grandfather
    Lavenus
       I never saw
          I have three images of him

He led the family band (was this French-Canadian custom I wonder, or just Lavenus?). He played the tuba, my Aunt Corinne played the piano, Ernest the trumpet, Sylvio the trombone, Clara the violin (not well). The others I don't know but they did play an instrument, it was a complete family band. Marcel on drums.

Another image; he was burned up in a fire (at his box-making plant I imagine)   taking leave of the family when the oldest boy was fifteen.

The third is my mother's memory of him. The children as a punishment had been put to bed without supper. It was upstairs in the Fairmont Avenue house where the four girls slept, barricaded with commodes. Looking out the window at the cherry tree in late afternoon summer light . . . Voices of the other kids playing on the street float up . . .
      Bitterness . . . When would Pappa be home? Easing the door gently, Lavenus tiptoed in late that night and smuggled them some supper.

          . .

And my own father
        where is he?
      holding my hand?

Was it mayflowers
he took me looking for in the wood?
   in the deep wood
with its litter of lodged beech leaves

        No   it was cowslips
     in the pasture
     It was
            marsh marigolds

Oh that leaping March wind!
ice breaking up on the lip
    of the meadow
the rimy edged pool

        Reaching for it I fell in . . .

And so soaked
& coming back in his car
   wrapped in a warm blanket
we were met by the first streetlights and dusk

      . . . waiting at the Marlborough Street R. R. crossing
        for the freight train to rumble by

          . .

    This poem
which I began (wrongly) 20 years ago
   (because I was unable to leave out anything)
I now complete
   in the small village of Tepotzlan Mexico 1982
for my own children

6 THE WEDDING

The announcement that my mother and father were to be married printed at the stationer's had been preceded by stormy scenes. Consternation on both sides. Neither family had met, and disliked each other on sight. To my grandfather, the vestryman at All Saint's Episcopal church (in his memory today there is a stained-glass window bathed in suffused light)   the invitation and subsequent car ride to Saint Joseph's Roman Catholic church on Grafton Street wounded like a whip and produced in Charles's sister and stepsisters a polite nausea. The party returned to the reception at Fairmont Avenue as if from a funeral.

I imagine my grandmother, my Grandmother Rose, and my Grandfather Charles's father staring at each other with dark hatred.

Though she knew some words of English she would not have used them then. It must be said—with the granite of the Breton or Normandy stone a part of her conviction—that all the other marriages of the children of Rose Lalone were to Catholics and French-Canadians. My Aunt Anita did not marry until she died (lived in the house with her). Ernest's marriage, the exception, to Anna, a Swede, was brief and tragic.

Grandmother Rose daubs her eyes with a handkerchief . . . The younger members of the family would have tried to lighten the occasion with what gaiety they had. There was wine but my grandfather's family were teetotalers. They stood around sourly. Ernest, now an army bugler, was away. But my father's younger brother—an airman on leave from France (he was killed soon after on the day of the armistice) was present and ready to have a good time. For him there was no difficulty in accepting Clara—who stood shining in her white dress by the window. He raised his glass, forcing his father and sisters to do the same. And made a toast.

Later as she left, my grandmother said to my mother: —You have made your bed. Now you must sleep in it.

7

It is the year 1915. A telephone operator's strike. The street is blocked off. The building is opposite City Hall. Sullen picketers. Angry cries . . . maybe snowballs are thrown. It is snowing. The scab operators come out (one of whom is my mother) and defiantly run the gauntlet on the sidewalk.

. .

Notice in the Worcester Telegram and Gazette Jan. 1916:

> "Help wanted. Personal secretary to insurance salesman. Must have bookkeeping experience."

The idea of my father, of course, selling insurance is ludicrous, but he did off and on for a few years. Later he would only wander enamored of escapes and trains. (I have described this is as poem on the long trainride.)

But now selling insurance in Worcester Mass. in a second floor office on Main Street at the insistence of his father, who set him up in an office with Lee Keith.

Clara among the twenty or thirty young women that day interviewed.

—I was at the end of the line, Clara recounted to her sisters. He came down the whole line looking awfully embarrassed. He interviewed them all and picked me.

It was a scream. Clara who knew no typing or shorthand, had no bookkeeping skills.

I can imagine Clara, sitting with him in the small office, come in to work the next day. And not hiding anything. Her eyes wide, a certain reckless bravura about her. I am what I am. After all it's not my fault I was hired.

Made friends with Lee Keith's secretary, and for weeks she did all her work for her.

Finally, hopelessly in love with her (in fact, without hope) Charles sent her to night school.

THREE POEMS

LARS GUSTAFSSON

Translated from the Swedish by Yvonne L. Sandstroem

BALLAD ON THE STONE FOREST IN YUNNAN

In the Province of Yunnan, two hundred forty *li*
southwest of the city of Kun Ming, where slow-moving
junks still sail solemnly
across emerald-green Lake Tien Chi
there's a vast forest made from stone.
Travelers of early dynasties
mention it with great respect, and in their words
an undertone of dread is often mingled,
as if they had seen something forbidden,
or something that perhaps ought not to be.
When Charlemagne was crowned in Rome,
when the deep-red color still glowed fresh
on the Pagoda of the Six Harmonies in Hang Chow,
far off beside another river,
ballads of this forest made from stone
were sung by men who'd walked or who'd been carried
in chairs across the two high mountain passes, along
the three rivers lining the road, through gorges
where this year the small green soldiers
of the People's Liberation Army still battle with

boiling engines of blunt-nosed trucks,
men naked above the waist drag timber of inhuman
proportions, laid on the handlebars of two bikes,
black pigs root in potholes in the asphalt,
the cyclists sound their monotonic bells,
men with springy steps are carrying burdens:
dried corn or human waste
in constant competition with their shadows
and the water buffaloes, in pairs, till
the meager deep-red fields, where someone has put down
rice to be thrashed by the wheels of passing trucks
right at the narrowest curve of the road.
It is this year: and we are still alive.
The forest is county-sized, incomprehensible,
no wind has moved its trees,
its tall pillars of black basalt,
the paths with ancient inscriptions
are lost in sharp-edged shadows, organ works
with pipes two hundred feet, where no one played,
icicles that never melt, a text
where the signs reach to heaven
and blot it out, a mournful text of stone
written long before man: and no one
will retract it. What does it say?
Sometimes the path cuts through tunnels, sometimes
it lightens, daylight glares sharply across bamboo brush,
a woman of the Dais, in curious dress,
plows a field large as a living room,
close by the pillars' roots, around the next corner
we no longer believe that she existed or
that she existed in the same time as ours,
and our watches run and show the same dead sign.
Deepest in the forest there's a river
whose black waters wash around black pillars,
in the deep forest spiders
have pitched gigantic webs. They've lived here a long time.
They're guardians of the forest. And they think other thoughts.
I'm forty-two years old, believe in nothing,
have tasted a little something of life,

without bitterness and without hope, railroad yards,
airports where the loudspeakers often change language,
the mighty libraries where lights play in the dust,
am somewhat acquainted with beauty: a drop of sweat
catching the light on the silken belly of a girl,
thunderstorms across lakes in Västmanland,
a mad dialogue of two flutes, *Adagio e piano*
in a trio sonata by Bach, where nothing
looks as if it would fit together, and yet it does.
The Master Li Ko Jan in Peking who's still alive
painted a *Landscape by the River Li*
where stones and water boundlessly mingle into each other,
he teaches us not to take stone too seriously,
not to take water too lightly; a different Master
who now lies dead in Peking, knows that the soft
can be hard and the hard be soft; in frost
keys break in the locks, the thawing wind moves the dams.
So many times when dust clouds rose
over the roads of China! So many swords! So many deaths!
But this text of stone was written by some man
for whom history never did exist
or perhaps by someone for whom everything existed
unchangeable, all in one moment.
If you look at the stones close up, there is a pattern,
something that might be a text
with signs from some language earlier than man.
Is the forest a library? Who did the writing?
Who writes us? Are there novels here
we haven't written yet? Epics on
the long marches that haven't yet begun?
Or is the forest about something else?
A text we aren't allowed to read, a message
from nonhuman to nonhuman
who ignore us and who tell us
that we were meaningless? And consequently free?
Thus gods do often speak, but never speak of us.
Now slanting shadows fall, wind passes through bamboo,
and across the river the western sky,
with a scent of smoke from fields and houses,
pulls its broad yellow tent. Who is writing us?

BALLAD ON THE RAIN HOUSES IN ENAMPOUR

In the great forest Oussoye,
beside the *baolong,* or tidal river,
which, to this day, the Diola men
call *Kamobeul,* in a surprising southern word,
there once ruled a king clad in red mantle, pointed red cap,
and with the broom-shaped scepter which testified
that he alone was the Spirit of that forest,
and he alone possessed the right to speak for it,
for all its holy trees, the gray hordes of baobabs,
and for his people of small black farmers
tending rice fields in narrow clearings between trees,
a people whose name's been lost forever.
This was long before the Almoravides
had found their way down to the Casamance River
broad and sluggish between Lapland shores,
long before the Portuguese slave ships
filled the shores with tears in dark Ziguinchor.
One day the King of Enampour
called all his ministers together
those representing the warrior caste
initiates of the secret arts that kill,
those representing smiths, sculptors, and singers,
those representing the free men,
those representing prisoners of war—
all of them assembled to the sound of stringed music
under his great royal council tree.
"Men, *griots,* ministers, artisans of Enampour!
Build me a house to keep the water from the rains
on earth, a house that will retain the past
even if only for a little while into the future,
in short, build for me, men of Enampour, a house
whose roof does not throw off the water of the rainy season
but gathers it in a basin for the use
of people and of animals, for drinking and for pleasant baths.
Because it cannot be the will of heaven
that the waters above me
shall run from the roofs, dissolving the red clay on our holdings.
Build a house for me, ye men, to keep the rains

on earth, a house that will retain the past,
giving it liberally to the future."
Ministers, warriors, artisans, and poets
were astounded by the depth of the riddle posed them.
And in a never-ending rain of leaves and branches
time in that forest fell upon them from great trees,
it was the clocks of trees that told them time was passing,
and underneath time's rain of leaves and branches they all
    pondered.
"Keeping the rain within a house on earth,"
said the wisest of the *griot* caste,
"is possible perhaps, perhaps it may be done,
perhaps one may keep too the lightning that strikes, the songs,
perhaps the storytellers' tales may be kept as well?
But the one who does it, always has to *lose* something."
For a long time, they built. They pondered, they tore down.
They pondered and rebuilt. They turned things inside out.
They did not know what might be lost.
After some days, no one knows how many, there it stood.
And they stand there still, in distant clearings
in the great forest Oussoye. They lean inward,
their roofs a funnel in a funnel emptying
into a basin in the middle of the house. People and goats
live around this well which is no well,
live in this lap which is no lap,
underneath this sky which is a narrowing funnel.
Strangely in double funnels life has turned inward,
for the people who followed the King of Enampour,
and what has been lost nobody knows.

THE EEL AND THE WELL

In old Scania there was a custom:
Into the deep old wells
young eels from the sea were dropped.
These eels stayed there all their lives

captive in the darkness of deep wells.
They keep the water crystal clear and clean.
When, at times, the eel comes up,
white, abominably large, caught in the pail,
blind, winding in and out
of his body's riddles, unknowing,
everyone hurries to lower him again.
I often feel I am
not just in place of the eel,
but well and eel at the same time.
Captive in myself, but this self
is already something different. I am there.
And I wash it with my coiling,
muddy, white-bellied presence in the dark.

WORK

DOUG CROWELL

I make my living washing drums, and there's always drums to wash. Every day the dirty drums come in on trucks, and every day I wash them. It's a good job. Some guys don't like it. Harold and R. J. and fat Charles all used to be on the drum-washer, but they got moved off it fast as they could. Me, I like it, being on the drum-washer, and I plan to stay as long as I have any say so about it. It's a good job, washing drums. And there's always dirty drums to wash. I don't really *wash* them, of course. It's all automatic. If I had to really get down and scrub them I likely wouldn't like it either, but it's all automatic, and I just get them ready to go is all. Drums come in on the trucks, I get them ready, push the buttons, and off they go. Clean drums. The job's all right. I mostly like it.

The two things I don't like about it are that there's no women around, and that the bosses don't seem to understand what it is I'm telling them. There is one woman at the plant, who works in the factory office, who's the secretary, but she's sort of old and dumpy and so the guys don't talk about her the way they would a younger, better-looking woman. I like her. We always get along, though I'm not in the office that much. She likes me too and that's easy to see, and so the guys kid me about that. She's a widow. The way they kid me means they like me, but still it gets old sometimes, gets pretty tiresome. They kid in the usual way, but that's all right, and I'm not going to let it keep me from being friendly to her. I like her. She walked by the lunchroom door one day just when someone was saying something. I know she heard it too, and so I was a little red-faced next time I had to go into the office, but she didn't seem to notice. I suppose she's used to it, though, working in a factory office instead of some other kind. I wonder sometimes what it was like for her when she was younger though, back when she was married.

The guys kid more about the women they can't have anyway, the married ones or the ones who come once in a while from the head office in Atlanta, to walk around the plant for a day or two. Those women make two, three times what we do, some of them. They do make that much, and I know some of the guys think about that sometimes. As soon as they walk in the plant we all know they're there and we all wonder what they look like underneath, those women who make that money. We know we could never have them, and so we kid about them a lot, the women who make that kind of money.

It's hard sometimes to get girls when you're only a drum-washer. I go pretty often down to the Cascade, to drink some beers and listen to the music. I know a couple of the bartenders pretty well, and usually a waitress or two, but they turn over pretty fast. The pay's not much. Two girls have been waitressing there ever since I've been going regular, and that's over a year. I wonder how they make it sometimes, or if they get money other ways. Maybe they get tips better than most. There are usually six bartenders there, even more on the busy nights. Maybe a dozen girls out doing tables. The Cascade's a big place, a big old-fashioned dance hall. Sometimes I do all right, sometimes I don't. Even when I do it's usually with a girl sort of like me, sourmouthed about one thing or another, and so the night never gets down to being too much fun. We mostly seem to just get drunker and drunker, and more and more sourmouthed, and nearly always I end up having to get out of their bed about the middle of the night and go back home to my own, all alone. That's not the way I want things to be, it sure isn't. I bet it's not the way they want things to be either, but neither of us seems to be able to do anything else.

The kind of girls I imagine could make me smile and laugh and have a good time are always the girls I can't get. Who don't want me. Every month the work in the office piles up for a day or two, and they hire a girl or two from the temporary help place. Mostly they're young and pretty, but they're not the kind of girls who would want me. The guys always kid about them though, and they wish on those days that they got to go into the office as much as I do. I go in to the main office now and then, because the drum-wash is close to the shipping office, and the guys up there are always getting me to carry down invoices and papers for the bosses to sign. It's not only because I'm close, but also because the drum-wash is about the only job that can be done pretty much at my speed and not at the speed of some machine or other. I come in earlier to work than all the other guys except for Herbie, who unloads trucks, and so I've always got two batches of drums washed by the time the other guys start working. We never run more than two batches before lunch and hardly ever more than one, so I can pretty much wash drums at my own speed once the other guys come in, and I'll still have more drums than we need for the day's run. The guys kid me about that sometimes, how I'm the man of leisure around the plant. So I end up doing a lot of odd jobs. I work hard those first two hours, but I can slack up after that, and I'd rather have it that way than have to go the same speed all day long like the guys on the machines do. So I get the hard part of my work done before the other guys get there, and then doing odd jobs now and then helps the day go by.

It's bad, though, in some ways. I know all the guys in the plant, but I don't know any of them very well because I don't really work *with* any of them. If you're on the drum-wash, you're pretty much off in the corner by yourself. Still, it's a good job. I get off at two-thirty instead of four-thirty like everyone else. I used to come back to the plant at four-thirty and go down with the guys to the Corner for a beer, but then I quit doing that. It's not the same when you don't get off at the same time. No one said anything, it was just different somehow, them just getting off work and me already out for two hours. So I quit going to the Corner, except now and then on Fridays. I like getting out early though, I like being out already while most people are still working. I don't go home right away, but I don't do anything with my time either. I like to go places and watch people. A cafeteria, or a coffee shop. For a while once I went downtown every day, to a cafeteria down there. I thought that maybe downtown would be different. It was in some ways.

Once I realized that someone had been watching me, someone I had not been seeing. One of the girls who worked there, cleaning tables, pushing the tea-cart around. One day she refilled my coffee cup and smiled at me and said hello. She'd been watching me, and I hadn't even known it. It was a funny feeling. Every day we talked a little, and finally I asked her out. She didn't seem sourmouthed like most girls with jobs like hers. I thought we might have a good time. Still, something seemed funny to me, so I didn't tell any of the guys I had a new girl lined up for Friday. When I went to pick her up, she lived with her parents, which she hadn't mentioned. I'd thought she was too old for that. Her father looked at me in a funny way, asked me about myself then seemed not to believe anything I said. Things seemed strange to me, but I thought it was only me, because I had not expected her to be living with her parents. We finally left, and I was glad to leave, glad to get away from her father's eyes. I just didn't know. We didn't go to the Cascade, but went to a quiet place instead, because we hadn't talked much. Not at all really, just her saying this or that and me smiling back, agreeing, when she came by with the tea-cart, or was cleaning off a table near me. And then I had asked her out. So there was no way I could know. It had never occurred to me. She seemed all right, but as we had a couple of drinks, it struck me she wasn't very smart. And it wasn't just that, it was something more. When the waiter came with our second drinks and looked funny at me out of one eye, I realized what it was he already knew, that I didn't yet know. Everything became clear. The girl was not only not smart, she was a retarded girl. She wasn't really bad, just a little bit, but that was enough. I wondered what the waiter thought. I had never known because it had never occurred to me. I guess I hadn't paid that much attention to her in the cafeteria. She was retarded, even if it was only a little bit. Everything was clear, the way her father had looked at me, why she wasn't sourmouthed.

There was nothing in her eyes, just nothing there. Otherwise, she looked and talked normal. She did. She had a job and was friendly to me, and I never noticed, not until the waiter looked at me the way he had. I didn't know what to do. We hadn't been gone an hour yet, I didn't want to take her home, but I didn't want to go anywhere with her. We left the bar, I bought beer, and we went to a drive-in movie, where no one could see us. I didn't know what to do. It crossed my mind to drive off when she went to the bathroom, but I couldn't do that. We drank the beer, and then I took her home. She wanted me to fool around with her, and once I started feeling her breasts. But I couldn't do it. I wondered how many guys went out with her, knowing. She seemed eager. It made me sad. She was normal looking except for her eyes, and unless she talked too long she only sounded not too smart, not retarded. She let me know that I could make her easy, but I couldn't. I felt funny. Her kisses were as blank as her eyes. I thought of Crazy Joe, a guy at work. He would have fucked her and left her and told us all about it at lunch on Monday. But I didn't tell anyone. We drank the beer, and I took her home. Her father was up and stared at me. I felt creepy. But when I was driving away I laughed out loud, and it was okay then. I even wondered what it might have been like. There was nothing in her eyes, nothing. I never went back to where she worked. I thought of her cleaning up tables, smiling and saying hello to guys sitting alone. She could smile because she just didn't know, didn't know anything. No wonder she hadn't been sourmouthed.

Girls think I don't know anything either, sometimes. I know they do. I try not to think about it. It's frustrating, thinking that, knowing that the bosses don't listen to me either. They won't say why they won't listen, and when I'm feeling bad it makes me wonder. It's like they know something I don't know, and never will. It makes me feel sometimes like I don't know anything. I make a suggestion about how the drum-wash, or some other job, could be done better, or faster, or easier. But they won't listen, they just smile and nod, and then things go on like always. Sometimes I do think they know something I don't, but good for me I don't feel that way too often, because it makes me feel bad. Makes me want to go get drunk. Makes me mad. The girls at the Cascade smile like that sometimes too. Sometimes I wonder why and sometimes I get mad and say, fuck you bitch, and sometimes I try to smile that smile back at them, but it never feels right. They do know something I don't, or seem to, or think they do. There's nothing wrong with me. What's the matter with washing drums?

Once I was sitting down the table from two girls who were pretty nice looking; they were laughing and talking and seemed up for a good time. I was trying to decide to go down the table to talk to them when some other guy beat me to it. So I listened. The three of them talked, and those girls seemed okay. I wanted to join in, I almost did. Especially when one girl went off to dance with that guy and left the other by herself. She looked at me but didn't smile. I pretended I hadn't seen. The other two came back in half an hour, and when the guy got up to go buy drinks, one girl asked, What does he do? and the other girl said, He works in a factory, he puts fans together. They laughed then, like that was funny. When he came back with the drinks they all kept on laughing, but the girls were laughing at him now. He didn't know it either, but he'd find out I knew, at night's end if not before. They wouldn't go home with him. I got up then and moved to another table. I hated those girls, and I almost hated myself.

Those are the kind of girls Crazy Joe says you gotta get 'em on their knees, like you're gonna screw 'em from behind, then fuck 'em through the back door. That'll teach 'em, he says. Crazy Joe was going to go to Canada once, way up north, and live by hunting with arrows. He took archery for six months to get ready, then came to work drunk one day with a two-hundred-dollar bow in his hand. He smashed that bow to pieces on the walls of the loading dock, crying all the time. His wife had left him. The bosses almost fired him but let him come back after he sobered up. Crazy Joe's okay, he's just a little off sometimes. Three days later he was back, talking about some sixteen-year-old hitchhiker he picked up somewhere. Jim says those are the kind of women you've got to forget about. They don't do anybody any good. I like Jim, we get along all right. The first week I was working we were talking down on the docks. I was waiting for more drums to come in. He was telling me about his son. I asked how old he was and Jim said seven, and I asked when his birthday was and Jim said January 1. Hell, I said, that's *my* birthday. Okay, Jim said, his is the 2nd then. Ever since we've gotten along just fine. I get along with everybody though, more or less, except for Doyce, and I get along with him too, in an odd sort of way. The first week I came to work, Doyce caught me on Friday afternoon and told me to come in to work the next afternoon. When I drove up on Saturday there was Doyce and a few of the other guys drinking beer in the parking lot, waiting for me to show up so they could laugh. I didn't mind much, I thought it was pretty funny myself, but there was just the wrong kind of edge to Doyce's voice. We had to fight, though neither of us wanted to. We both bled a little,

Doyce bled a little more than me, and ever since there's been something a little off between us. There haven't been any problems, but we don't get along real well. We both get along real well with Jim, but neither of us cares much of anything about the other. The beer we drank in the parking lot that afternoon was the only beer we ever drank together. We don't kid each other much either. Hardly at all.

Sometimes I wonder if I want too much, if I'm asking too much. I don't have a lot to offer in some ways, but I'm a good guy. I could do right by a girl. I want a girl who's not sourmouthed, but it seems sometimes that the only girls I can get are the tight-lipped ones. We're all in the same boat. I try not to be that way myself, but sometimes I can't help it. I work hard and don't get much of anywhere, and probably won't. What can I do? The girls that I want want better than me. The girls I can get scare me sometimes, they're so hard. What can I do? Once I was at the Cascade, sitting at a back table alone, and one of the waitresses I liked came and sat at the table behind me, on her break. Another waitress joined her. They were talking about all the lonely girls, all the lonely guys who were at the place that night. If only the guys would realize, I heard the one I liked say, that all they have to do is just go up and say hello. It's not that easy, I thought, it doesn't work like that, and you, you work here, you should know better. You should. I wanted to tell her that, I wanted to turn around and say it. She should know better. If I had turned around and said hello to her, she would have stopped me cold, I knew, because I had seen her be approached before. She wanted better. But would she have seen the point I wanted to make? No. It's not that easy, and she, she worked there, she should know better. She should.

Mostly when I come to the Cascade I come alone. Sometimes I bring a girl but not too often. I like the fact that I'm always alone, ready for anything to happen. I feel better that way. The Cascade *means* being alone, to me. Sometimes I wonder why I like the place the way I do. Watching the people, talking to the bartenders, looking at girls. It's hard to say the way I like it, the Cascade. Even when the girls say no, it's just part of the place, for me. It's the Cascade.

One time at work one of the women from the head office forgot some papers she had brought along. It was a Friday. I was caught up on the drums, so the foreman asked me to take the company car and drive her back to her motel. Usually three or four come at a time, but this time this woman had come by herself. I recognized her, she had been there before a few times. She seemed nice. On the drive over she asked me about the plant, about my job, about the people I worked with. I answered her. She picked up the papers from her room. On the drive back she asked me more about me, what I liked, what I did, where I went in town. Things like that. I mentioned the Cascade to her, said a little about it, about the music mainly. When I told her I mostly went alone, she seemed surprised. Then she asked if I might take her there. She said she would like to see the place. I didn't know what to think, whether she was kidding me or not, playing with me or not. She made a lot more money than me, but she had been friendly, so I said sure. I picked the woman up that night at her motel room, not sure how I should act. She made more money than I did by a long shot. She was smarter than I was. She was dressed too much for the Cascade. But she had a bottle in her room, and she asked me in for a drink, and she was friendly, and I started to think I might have a good time after all. She wasn't sourmouthed at all. She smiled at me. She talked to me. I didn't want her to ask about me, so I asked about her. She told me about herself. We had another drink. She had gone to school three different places, and had lived in three others. She'd been to Mexico once, and to Canada. One time she had even lived in Greece, seeing ruins and living on an island. I hadn't been anywhere. I had only seen postcards or pictures of all those places. She made three times what I did. But all the way through she was friendly to me. I even started talking to her, different from the way I usually talked to women.

On the way to the Cascade and then when we got there, she mostly asked about me. Or about the Cascade, why I went there, what I liked about it. She liked it too. She was surprised at the size, inside. It didn't look so big from outside. She didn't know much about the kind of music they played there but she said she liked it better than she would have thought. We danced a lot. We drank a lot of beers. In between dancing, I started telling her things, things I knew but hadn't ever thought much about. She seemed interested and kept on asking me more about things. I told her about my bartender friend, T. Paul, who played music and hoped some day to get in with one of the bands who played the Cascade. There were some big-name bands who played there. T. Paul nearly always got to play a few songs with the band, and they would usually let him have a little solo too. T. Paul was known. But T. Paul played flute. There wasn't much room for a full-time flute player in the bands who played the Cascade. T. Paul knew that, but I never asked him what he thought about it. He kept on working the bar and playing whenever they'd let him get up there with them. He could make that flute fit into any kind of music. T. Paul could play, he could play his flute.

I told her about the waitress I knew who made quilts and sold some of them at shows. She had even won a prize one time, or an award. I pointed out things going on in the Cascade. Nothing much, but she seemed interested. I would point out a guy going up to a girl and tell her what was going to happen, how the girl would act, stuff like that. I was always right. I pointed out people who were always at the Cascade. I told her stories about the night they did this, or that. I had her laughing. She said I must know a lot about people, but I told her I didn't know anything, that all I did was watch. Just watch. And somehow, thinking about myself watching, it made me feel funny. She noticed, and asked me what the matter was. I said nothing, tried to snap out of it. But she knew that something had happened to me. I knew it too, but there was no way for me to say what it was. She said we should go, I said sure. I didn't feel bad, I just felt funny. I was thinking about myself always watching.

I never even thought about how I was going to say good-bye to her. I was thinking about myself too much. When we got back to her room she asked me if I wanted to come in for another drink, and I said all right. I wasn't thinking about anything. The ice in the plastic bucket had melted. While she went out to get more, I stood in the middle of her motel room and looked around me. Some of her clothes lay neatly across one of the two beds in the room. Her suitcase cost a lot of money. It sat on one of the chairs in the room with the top open and lying up against the back of the chair. I had never seen a packed woman's suitcase before. The things inside looked soft to me. On the desk were the papers from her work, the ones we had driven back for. She came in then, with a bucket full of ice and a smile for me. She shut the door and fastened the chain. I wasn't thinking of anything though, nothing at all.

She poured two drinks, and sat down on the bed her clothes were on. I sat in a chair across from her. I felt my lower lip quiver then. I hadn't known it was going to. She looked at me and said if there was something I wanted to talk about, she would be glad to listen. I believed her, and wanted to talk, but I didn't know what I wanted to say. It was then I began to break. Because she had said such a simple, kind thing. I started telling her things I hadn't known to say until I said them. She seemed to understand. I was about half crying. I told her how it seemed I couldn't have even the simple things I wanted. I told her how I hated the way I felt sometimes, of not being able to do anything, or to have anything, of being always on the outside. I told her how the bosses never listened. I tried to tell her why I fought Doyce. I told her about the women at the Cascade. I was crying out loud. I couldn't stop. I tried to tell her everything, but I knew she wouldn't know the half of it. She might be friendly, be kind, but she just wouldn't know. She couldn't know. She came and put her arms around me though. She took me to her bed. I was crying out loud. I wasn't thinking about anything. I was just crying, trying to talk in between the deep breaths I had to take. I started telling her about something that had happened to me once, at the Cascade. I don't know why it came back to me then. I talked, trying to think about what I was saying. She kept saying yes, yes, and put her hands on me. I tried to tell her, and she began to take my clothes off.

I had gone to the Cascade one night, and when I got there I saw a girl who was really attractive. Before I realized what I was letting happen to me, I was telling myself that I had to have her. She was beautiful. I had never seen the girl before. She was with friends, a couple, but she was by herself. She was too good for me, I could tell. There was something about her though that I really wanted. When I see a girl like her I usually forget about it, but this girl attracted me so strongly that while her friends were dancing, I went to talk to her. She let me buy her a drink, but she didn't listen to me. When her friends came back it was like I wasn't even there. She ignored me. It's happened to me before, but it never bothers me much. This time it did, I don't know why. When I got up from her table and left, I felt that everyone in the Cascade was watching me. I went to the far end of the place and sat by myself at one of the small round tables in the back. All around me were couples talking, but I sat alone and brooded. I tried to laugh but couldn't. I tried to think but couldn't.

I sat and drank beer all night. I got mad. I never moved from that table, not once. I didn't notice anything all night. A little after midnight the girl's friend came and sat at my table. When I looked up and saw her there I hated her. She told me her friend was real drunk and wanted to leave, but she and her boyfriend didn't want to leave yet. She asked me to give her friend a ride home. I hated her more. I hated her, but I said that I would. I was drunk too. The girl and I left the Cascade. She fell down twice on the way to the car. I put my arm around her to help. She was drunker than I was, and I had been drinking to brood. When she got into my car she passed out, fell right asleep. She lived a long way off. I took the long way to get there, taking streets instead of the freeway. I found myself touching her whenever I stopped for a red light. She never knew it. The closer we got to her house the bolder I got. I felt her thighs. I felt her breasts. I rubbed her crotch. I put my hand inside her knit top, rubbed her belly, her breasts. She was beginning to come out of her drunk. She touched me back, but I knew she wasn't fully awake. I would stay stopped through half a dozen light changes, touching her, rubbing her. I never kissed her. When we got to the address her friend had given me, she said it wasn't her house but her friend's. They lived in a rich part of town. She said she was too drunk yet to drive home. I said I'd take her there. She said she couldn't go home without her car, her father would not like it. She said she'd stay with me until she could drive. We sat in my car, on the street in front of a very rich house. I wanted her. No matter the way she had treated me earlier, I wanted her. I hated her too, because I wanted her like that. As she came out of her drunk, she touched me, rubbed me. She was smiling, but I knew what it meant. She was playing with me, I knew that, but I let her do it, because I wanted her so much. I was nothing to her, not anything. I felt ashamed of myself, for letting her do it. I could never touch her. She would let me do anything I wanted to her, and it wouldn't matter, because I was nothing to her. Nothing. She wasn't even seeing me, and I knew that, yet I wanted her, still. I touched her body. I took her knit top off and bent to kiss her breasts, and all she did was smile that smile. I hated her, and I hated myself, but still I took her pants off. Her smile kept on saying, you can't touch me, you could never touch me, you're nothing. And I wanted her so much that I did it, fucked her, and I hated myself after. I hated her too, and her friend who had given her to a stranger to take her home. They were careless people. And they could be as careless as they wanted, because I was nothing to them. And they knew that even I knew that. But I had wanted her, and I had fucked her, and I had hated myself after.

I told my story to the woman from Atlanta, and when I finished I was on my back in her bed. She was on top of me and moving, and I put my arms over my face, and I was yelling at her, what's the matter with me, is there anything the matter, what is it that's the matter, what's wrong with me, and she was moving above me and saying as she moved, nothing, not anything, there's nothing the matter, nothing wrong with you, not at all, nothing.

The next day she flew back to Atlanta, and the next time she came to the plant with the others, it was as though she had never known me before, as though I had not shown her me, myself. I washed drums, and she walked by.

HWÆT!

Five American Modernist Poets in Old English Translation

JAMES LAUGHLIN · DENISE LEVERTOV · GEORGE OPPEN · KENNETH REXROTH · GARY SNYDER

Translated and introduced by Peter Glassgold

"Make it new." Ezra Pound's watchword for modernism proclaimed the poets' discarding of the self-consciously "poetical." Free verse ought to be free from the bounds of traditional forms and arbitrary language and the need of set classical allusions for meaning. Let the sense of the poem be carried purely in its words.

Theoretically, poems with such purity of language should be easily translatable. Could they even be translated back in linguistic time? I became curious to find how some of my favorite poems in the modernist mode, by Pound and Williams Carlos Williams (see *Modern Poetry in Translation 1983*, Persea Books), as well as other, later poets, might sound in the English of a thousand years ago.

The translations here do not draw on the Old English poetic tradition, which was highly stylized. I have tried to use what it seems to me must have been words in everyday speech. Where they were lacking in the historical record, I made them up: word-formation in Old English comes naturally. *Maca hit niwe.*

A Note on the Title and a Few Words about Spelling and Pronunciation

Hwæt! is the cry—usually rendered "lo!"—that opens such Old

English poems as *The Dream of the Rood* and *Beowulf*. It can also mean "what," "who," and "quick."

The phonetic values of Old English letters seem to have been the same as in Latin. There were some special signs, of which only the "thorn" (Þ, þ) is used here. It represents the Modern English "th" combination, both voiced and unvoiced—as in "*th*is" and "*th*in." Þ was voiced between vowels and between a vowel and another voiced consonant. It was unvoiced in all other positions and when doubled. The letters *f* and *s* were likewise voiced (as in our *v* and *z*) or unvoiced.

R was trilled at the beginning of a word and otherwise sounded emphatically, as in Dutch and American Midwestern pronunciation.

The letters *c* and *g* had both a hard (*k*, *g*) and soft (*ch*, *y*) pronunciation, not readily determined, though modern forms often serve as guides. In any case, the soft manner is printed here as *ċ* and *ġ*. The combination *cg* was a voiced *ċ* (as in fu*dg*e). *Sc* was generally pronounced in a soft manner (*sh*ip). The occasional hard sound (a*sk*, *sc*hool), once again, follows modern usage in the main.

H initially or in combination (*hw*, *hl*, *hr*) was always pronounced, and with the modern breathing sound. Otherwise, it was gutturalized, as in German and Scots.

In general, Latin or Italian usage seems the best approximation for vowels. The combination æ in Old English, however, was pronounced pl*ay* when long and *at* when short. In diphthongs, the emphasis was on the first vowel.

Stress was generally on the root element or the first syllable if it was not a prefix, as in English today and all other Germanic languages.—PG

JAMES LAUGHLIN

HIT DEÞ ME TO GODE

to bugenne min bodiġ to þæm grunde
þaþa se casere oferfærþ iċ eom

ortġeardwearda an æt þæm
caserhame bute iċ ne ġeseah næfre

his ansien þaþa he gæþ on þæm
ortġearde he is foregan be ġeonglingum

þa þe hringaþ lytla bellan and iċ
buge me selfne ofdune þaþa iċ

hiere þa bellan nealæċende þeah-þe
hie secgaþ þæt se casere sie

swiþe milde and na eaþe ne ge-
bolgen he moste hliehhan on me

ġif iċ locie up oþþe furþum sprecan
to me bute iċ geliefe þæt se

casere ricsaþ be minre eaþmodnesse
min eaþmodnes self heo ricsaþ.

The original poem, "It Does Me Good," reads: "to bow my body to the ground / when the emperor passes I am / one of the gardeners at the / palace but I have never seen / his face when he walks in the / garden he is preceded by boys / who ring little bells and I / bow myself down when I hear / the bells approaching though / they say that the emperor is / very kind and not easily of- / fended he might smile at me / if I look up or even speak / to me but I believe that the / emperor rules by my humility / it is my humility that rules." **orġeardwearda an:** literally, "of the orchardwarders one." **be geonglingum: by boys.** The word "boy" and its alternative "lad" are Middle English (ME) and of unknown origin. The word "smile," too, first appeared in ME, but derived from a Germanic root common to many languages. Thus, **smile at me** becomes **hliehhan on me:** literally, "laugh [i.e., pleasantly] on me." **min eaþmodnes self heo ricsaþ:** literally, "my humility herself she rules."

Denise Levertov

MÆRE FOREGENGAN

Se Rabbi
of Norþerne Hwitre Russie nolde,
on his ġeogoþe, to leornienne þæt
fugliscan ġereord, for þæm þe
se uterra ne beheold him; swaþeah
þaþa he wearþ eald man funde
he understod hie æġhwæs,
hlysnende wel, and swa man sæġþ, 'ġebiddende
          mid þære benċe and þære flora.' He breac
swa hwæs swa wæs to handa—swa dyde
Enġel Jones of Molde, þæs smeanga
siwoda wæron on haman and breċ.
      Wel, hit wolde licaþ me to scieppenne,
þenċende sumu line þa ġiet togen between me and him,
scopleoþ on ġerihte swaswa hwæt þa fuglas sæġdon,
heard swaswa flora, ġesund swaswa benċe,
ġerynelicu swaswa þære stilnesse þaþa se seamere
wolde blinnan mid his nædle on þære lyfte.

The original poem, "Illustrious Ancestors," reads: "The Rav / of Northern White Russia declined, / in his youth, to learn the / language of birds, because / the extraneous did not interest him; nevertheless / when he grew old it was found / he understood them anyway, having / listened well, and as it is said, 'prayed / with the bench and the floor.' He used / what was at hand—as did / Angel Jones of Mold, whose meditations / were sewn into coats and britches. / Well, I would like to make, / thinking some line still taut between me and them, / poems direct as what the birds said, / hard as a floor, sound as a bench, / mysterious as the silence when the tailor / would pause with his needle in the air." **Se Rabbi:** "The Rabbi"—as in the Old English (OE) Gospel of St. John. The word *rav*, meaning "great one," originally the title of respect for Talmudic scholars in the late Babylonian Jewish community, was adopted by

40 HWÆT!

the Hasidim of Eastern Europe for their wise men and community leaders. The more commonly known term *rabbi* was the Palestinian equivalent of *rav* and means, simply, "my great one." **nolde**: *ne wolde*. That is, "did not wish." **man funde: it was found**: literally, "one found." Similarly, **swa man sægþ: as it is said. to scieppenne . . . scopleoþ: to make . . . poems**: literally, "to shape [create] . . . poet-songs." OE *scop* means "poet." **ġerynelicu: mysterious**. From OE *run* ("rune"). **wolde blinnan: would pause**.

GEORGE OPPEN

GEONGLINGES BUR

Sum freond seah þa buras
Keatses and Shelleyes
Æt þæm mere, and seah 'hie wæron efne
Geonglinga buras' and wæs onstyred

Be þæm. And huru scopes bur
Biþ ġeonglinges bur
And iċ wene þæt wifmenn cnawaþ hit.

Wenunga se unfæġera mynetere
Is onhætende to wifmenn, mann
Na ġeongling pyffende
For æþme ofer mæġdenċildes bodiġe.

The original poem, "Boy's Room," reads: "A friend saw the rooms / Of Keats and Shelley / At the lake, and saw 'they were just / Boys' rooms' and was moved / By that. And indeed a poet's room / Is a boy's room / And I suppose that women know it. / Perhaps the unbeautiful banker / Is exciting to a woman, a man / Not a boy gasping / For breath over a girl's body." Title: **"Geonglinges Bur": "Boy's Room"**: that is, "Youngling's Bower." **wene . . . . Wenunga: sup-**

pose .... **Perhaps.** Both words have the root sense of hope/
thought/expectation. **mynetere: banker.** A "moneychanger" or
"minter."

KENNETH REXROTH

DELIA REXROÞ

California wielcþ on
Slæpiġne sumor, and seo lyft
Is full þæs biteran swetan
Smocan of þæm græsfyrum biernendum
Ofer þa San Franciscan hyllas.
Flæsc biernþ swa, and þa enta ġeweorc
Ġeliċe, and þa biernendan steorran.
Teorod toniht, on byriġ
Becumendra manna, on þæm unmenniscum
Westdæle, on þæm mæst bloddrenċedan ġeare,
Iċ tac ofdune boc of scopleoþum
þe licode þe æror, þe þu
Wolde singan mid gliwe iċ ne
Næfre funde eft nahwær—
Michael Fieldes boc, *Lange Agan.*
Huru hit is lange agan nu—
Þin ærene hær and swancore bodiġ.
Iċ telle þu wære strangu lufestre,
Wilde wif, nietenlicu
Modor. And nu lif stod
Me maran ġear, þeah miċle læsse sar
Þonne þu scolde ġieldan for him.
And iċ bohte onbæc, for and of
Me selfum, þas scopleoþ and fæhunga,
Corfen of uncweþendum bane,
Þa dieran wyrde
Of þinum torenan and unstillan life.

42 HWÆT!

The original poem, "Delia Rexroth," reads: "California rolls into / Sleepy summer, and the air / Is full of the bitter sweet / Smoke of the grass fires burning / On the San Francisco hills. / Flesh burns so, and the pyramids / Likewise, and the burning stars. / Tired tonight, in a city / Of parvenus, in the inhuman / West, in the most blood drenched year, I took down a book of poems / That you used to like, that you / Used to sing to music I / Never found anywhere again— / Michael Field's book, *Long Ago*. / Indeed it's long ago now— / Your bronze hair and svelte body. / I guess you were a fierce lover, / A wild wife, an animal / Mother. And now life has cost / Me more years, though much less pain, / Than you had to pay for it. / And I have bought back, for and from / Myself, these poems and paintings, / Carved from the protesting bone, / The precious consequences / Of your torn and distraught life." **Slæpiġne**: the accusative case. *Slæpiġ* is not recorded in OE, but *unslæpiġ*, "sleepless," is. **þa enta ġeweorc**: literally, "the work of giants," a frequent OE phrase for ancient ruins (cf. *The Wanderer*, l. 87). The word "pyramid" is not recorded until the fourteenth century. It is derived from the Greco-Latin *pyramis* and is of uncertain meaning and origin. **strangu . . . wilde . . . nietenlicu: fierce . . . wild . . . animal. stod: has cost**: literally, "has stood." **fæhunga: paintings.** From *fæhan*, to "paint." **Þa dieran wyrde: The precious consequences**: literally, "the dear fates."

GARY SNYDER

BE FRAZIERES BROCES WÆTERGEFEALLE

Standende uppe ofer hafenum, fealdenum stanrocce
lociende ut and ofdune—

Se broc fielþ to sumum feorrum dæle.
hyllas beġeondan þæm
toweard, healf-wudufæstede, dryġe
—leohtre lyfte

strang wind on þæm
stifan glisniendan nædlclystrum
þara pintreowa—hiera brunu
sinewealtu stemn-bodiġ
rihtu, stillu;
swogendu cwaciendu limu and twigu

hlyste.

Þis libbende flowende land
is eall þæt is, æfre

We *beoþ* hit
hit singþ þurh us—

We meahton libban ofer þisse Eorþe
wiþutan claþum oþþe tolum!

The original poem, "By Frazier Creek Falls," reads: "Standing up on lifted, folded rock / looking out and down— / The creek falls to a far valley. / hills beyond that / facing, half-forested, dry / —clear sky / strong wind in the / stiff glittering needle clusters / of the pine—their brown / round trunk bodies / straight, still; / rustling trembling limbs and twigs / listen. / This living flowing land / is all there is, forever / We *are* it / it sings through us— / We could live on this Earth / without clothes or tools!" **healf-wudufæstede: half-forested:** literally, "half-woodfast," derived from *wudufæsten,* meaning "forest covering," "forest stronghold," or in poetical metaphor, "ship." **sinewealtu: round.** It is interesting that the Old French *rond-* displaced what must have been common expressions of native stock denoting roundness in all Germanic languages. **swogendu cwaciendu: rustling trembling:** literally, "soughing quaking."

A YOUNG WOMAN'S WINTER NIGHT

WILLIAM HOLINGER

Something woke her during the night. When she opened her eyes she was lying on her back, and the room was so dark she couldn't see. She lay still, listening for the sound that had wakened her. But she heard nothing. The winter night was silent.

From far away, suddenly, came the muted sound of squealing automobile tires. That was all, just a long, wrenching squeal, preceded by nothing, followed by nothing. The sound was entirely disconnected from everything—the silence, the darkness—and it seemed to have carried a long way before it reached the farm.

Surely that's not what woke me up, she thought.

After the sound faded, the bedroom felt even more still to her than it had before. She drew in a deep breath and let it out slowly. The sound of her sigh filled the quiet darkness of the room, as if with light, and then she realized what had wakened her: the silence. She could not hear her husband breathing.

She lay still for a long moment, waiting for him to resume breathing. Does it have to be tonight? she thought. Does it have to be now?

He lay beside her, on his back, his left arm (the one near her) stretched alongside him, his hand resting palm down. He always lay that way.

She remained still and listened. She listened for him to draw a breath, or to stir, or to talk in his sleep. She listened without straining, for he lay right next to her; she listened for any sound, listened for phlegm to catch in his throat, for him to cough or choke, for him to groan or cry out. But he neither moved nor made a sound.

Cautiously, beneath the blankets, she slid her hand toward his. She touched his fingers. They were not cold. She touched his palm, felt the fleshy padding near his fingers. That skin had once been hard with callouses. Now it was soft, and loose. She poked the middle of his palm with her forefinger, but he did not respond. It was an old habit: she would touch his hand, and he would give her fingers a squeeze. Even in his sleep, if she touched him, he would find her hand and squeeze it. He had done it from the time they'd begun to sleep together, a few weeks before they married. But this time there was no answering pressure from his thick fingers.

Now she knew that he must have stopped breathing just moments before, and a burning feeling spread through her, a kind of fear. What should I do? she thought. Should I call someone? Who should I call?

She moved a little away from him, carefully, trying not to jiggle the bed. She didn't want to disturb him. Then she realized that her caution made no sense, that he would not wake up. She could not possibly disturb him, because he was dead.

So it's happened, she said to herself. He's been dying for a long time. All that pain, and now he's finally dead.

He'd been sick for nearly a year. When she first heard about his cancer, she was devastated. She had fainted in the waiting room of the clinic, and it had taken the doctor a few moments to revive her. She remembered wanting not to regain consciousness.

It seemed as though they'd just begun. They'd been married for six years, and had owned the farm for only three. They had been talking about a family. One of the first things they'd done after the disease was diagnosed was start trying to have a child, but she had not conceived.

For a while, too, she'd been enraged at him. How could he die on her like this? How could she possibly run the farm alone and attend to a dying man at the same time? She felt deserted, and she resented all the care he began to require. But after a couple of months, her anger passed.

What would she feel next, she wondered, now that he was actually dead? She felt only a kind of blankness. But there was also an anxiety, a fear of what would come next.

She reached up and touched her breast. Then she slipped her hands inside her nightgown, arms crossed, a hand on each breast. She remembered when they first had begun to grow; she'd never been so embarrassed about anything in her life. Men didn't look at her face anymore, or keep their eyes on her eyes when they talked to her. They looked down at her breasts! She'd been so humiliated. And when he first touched them, she thought she'd die. She was ashamed because she wanted him to. And he'd touched them again, last night, when she got into bed next to him.

How long till morning? She didn't know what time it was, but she felt that dawn was still a long way off. The sun rose late this time of year.

The silence of the winter night was beginning to disturb her. She wished there were noises she could listen to. In the summer it never used to trouble her to awake during the night; in summer she could hear the hogs outside, hear the leaves of the tall corn plants brush against one another, hear the warm rain, hear the crickets and cicadas, hear the oak leaves stir with every breath of wind. Those were gentle sounds. They drifted in easily through the window screens, and they always comforted her when she awoke late on a summer night.

But in winter those sounds were gone. The house was shut up tight with storm doors and storm windows. The hogs had been locked away in the shed, and the corn had been reaped, shredded, and stored in the silo. Most of the leaves were gone from the oaks in the yard. She had raked up every one of the dry oak leaves herself, made a pile, and burned them. She could hear the trees now only during a winter storm, when their frozen branches clicked against one another like bones, and their trunks creaked and groaned and threatened to split. When a branch came down—she heard that. She heard it crack like a rifle shot and she awoke instantly, and then she waited to see if it would crash through the roof or a window.

That was how she felt now: as if some strong wind had broken off not a mere branch, nor even a whole tree, but *all* the trees—every one of those huge burr oaks in the front yard—and had brought them crashing to the ground.

Well, she thought, we saw it coming a long way off. He was ready, and I guess I was too. If I can get through tomorrow, I'll be all right. But I'll need my rest. And it's not time for him to go, not just yet. I'll stay with him a while.

She nestled down farther under the covers. She started to reach out her hand toward him, but then she thought better of it. She turned over, away from her dead husband, and went back to sleep.

She saw him in a dream. He was standing in the alfalfa pasture, in summer, and he stood tall and straight. The alfalfa came almost to his knees. He was wearing a white T-shirt and his red Massey Ferguson hat. He was not smiling, but he looked healthy—ruddy and cheerful. Her fear left her. He hadn't looked that good alive, not in the last four months. She was happy for him.

Then she awoke. It was just past daybreak, and she knew she'd be all right. She looked over at him, and she could see that the thing next to her in bed was not him but was something else. It was not him. He was somewhere else, and she was going to be all right. Then she heard herself moan, and she knew she would not be all right. She could not face the day by herself; she would rather die too. She did not want to wake up and she did not want to get up. She would stay in bed and go with him. She closed her eyes and immediately felt better. She began to feel as if she were drifting off to sleep. She longed to see him again. Perhaps he would come and ask her to go with him. She longed for him to come back and take her with him. She dreaded being alive, and he had looked so happy in her dream that she wanted to be with him. She tried to go back to sleep. She tried to conjure up his image again, but she could not. She wasn't sleepy now. She lay in bed for a long time until she heard a car in the driveway and the dogs started to bark. Then she sat up, turned her back to the thing in the bed, pulled off her nightgown, and began to dress.

EIGHT POEMS

J. B. GOODENOUGH

BRIDE

You are in my country.
If you dream of the home fields
The grain will blacken there;
If you remember the orchards
The apples will rot and drop.

You are mine now.
If you look for your mother
I will put out her eyes;
If you cry for your father
I will cut out his tongue.

I will get a child on you.
You will hold his face
To your face like a mirror;
You will see me in it.
And I will see you.

You will grow old here
Having found no water
Deep enough for drowning;
Having found no tree
High enough for hanging.

MASKED BALL

Once was a masked ball to
Which everyone in the village
Came, dressed as someone else
In the village, and life
Went on as usual next day:

But the butcher shoed
The horses, the smith buried
The dead, the gravedigger
Brewed ale, and all there was
To do got done somehow;

And in the bed my lady
Turning in heavy sleep
Lifted her face to me,
But in her belly carried
A child that was not mine.

I went to the priest, knelt
To the priest. He told me
It was good weather for
Planting, what with the south
Wind and the moon waxing.

OUTBUILDINGS

Better to set fire to them
Than to watch them fall,
The barn and the two sheds.

Years he had watched them
Lean inward on themselves,
Heard the beams cracking.

Beyond the fences he saw
Trees take over the tilted
Fields that bore no son.

And the lofts empty, stalls
That the wind blew clean:
Better to set fire to them.

One night he did it. Birds
Flew from the burning barn
With flame on their wings.

LOVERS RECALLED

Remembered, they stand
Turned toward the same
Corner of the mind,
Half-hidden in mist rising
From the still grass.

My hands smell of rye,
Clover, timothy;
I listen for the sound
Of an old bell
Across the field,

Like the farmer
Who was fond of the herd,
Who butchered gently,
Who never used
The same name twice.

HILL COUNTRY

If I wear a white dress
The snowy owl will choose me,
I will be the owl's bride.
You will hear the mouse shriek
In the baled hay at night.
Brown spots will dry on your step.

If I wear a black dress
The crow will claim me,
I will be the crow's lady.
The runt hedge-kitten will scream
Once, at daybreak. You will
Find some of it by noonday.

I will be a good wife.
I will put on any dress
You like. If you will take me.

AMONG VINES

Wisteria ties the roof
Of the porch down; morning-
Glory anchors the mailbox;
Green peas keep the garden
Fence from taking off.

Trumpet vine has locked
Up the front door that
We never used anyway;
Clematis tries now
To seal the back door.

Benign root and tendril,
They mean no harm.

I too know a hundred ways
Of holding on. And
No way of letting go.

DREAM CIRCUS IN RAIN

    (*I am going to run away*)
The tent leaks, the water
Puddles underfoot, reflecting rain
But no stripes, banners, tinsel.
    (*To join the circus.*)
The acrobats are too fat
To fly, the clowns can no longer
Find their real faces.
    (*Fine, said my mother,*)
The tiger died six towns
Ago; now two dwarves pace
Tandem in the sagging skin.
    (*What are you going to be?*)
They have eaten the white pony:
Maria Elena snaps her whip
And rats slide under hoops.
    (*I don't know, I said,*)
Down the road the colors of
The posters run, the posters peel
Dripping from the barn walls.
    (*Maybe the lion.*)

TIME BEFORE

Mine is the hollow time
Before the root learns
The trunk is severed;

Before brown minnows
Downstream hear beavers
Have dammed the brook;

Before the bees
In the pear-orchard see
Snow blooming in May sky;

Before my mouth
Calling your name knows
You have cut out my tongue.

NEAKHANIE, '82

A Six-part Journal

CAROL JANE BANGS

1
Cancer, she says, here.
Placing her hands
under her breasts,
lifting them like goblets.
No one told me
the body, too,
gets out of bounds like
children or lovers
who don't understand.
One day the small cells shift
in their honeycombs of salt,
lean toward the light
like sun-starved leaves,
thickening like thumbs.
No word to hold them back
once the tide has tasted land,
the wind stuck its
nose in the hedge.
The beach is littered
with translucent cadavers
that once lived,

as we do now,
by subtle adjustment
and jellyfish nerve.
These dimples are not
from smiling, she says,
smoothing the rumpled
pillows of skin.
When the goblets are gone
where will we pour the wine?
Not listening now
for any answer, turning
her head toward the chugging sea,
neck veins pulsing blue
as the incoming tide.
From the bag I have brought
I lift ripe peaches,
placing them one by one
on the deep green plate.

2
"I didn't believe it
until I heard the name."
Only with words do we feel
the extravagance of pain;
the word "saffron"
rides on the tongue,
a rich biscuit,
bumblebees gilded
with drowsy pollen.
"Crocus" is an opening,
light, a fist unclenching,
pale fingers reaching
toward a dangling peach,
September wakings,
the sun daybreak red.
We teach our children
the proper vowels,
opening wounds of

frustrated love
no alphabet will salve.
Looking up they say
"cloud," "weather,"
where before they drifted
under the surface,
reflections of themselves.
One by one the mouth attempts
anger, pity, devotion,
emotions accreting like
oystershell, nacre,
mother-of-pearl spit
out between the teeth:
"I want no dish that is broken."

3
"I never liked mirrors,"
she says, standing naked,
"all this too much on one side."
As she touches eyelid,
nipple, thigh, she
names them as a mother
teaches an infant,
placing the body in the air
one piece at a time.
"One should know oneself
from the inside out,
not the other way.
When I first made love
to a man I saw
my breasts in his hands
like dough, kneaded
and worked that way,
and they didn't seem
to be mine anymore.
When the baby sucked
his mouth pulled so tight
I thought he'd draw

my whole body in
one piece at a time,
but then he'd let go,
all at once, his mouth
corners drooling milk,
the nipples would snap back
into the flesh, elastic,
blue as plums.
Sometimes I wanted to
take them off, overfull,
blue-veined udders.
Empty, they hung on my chest
like the waterbags old cars
slung over their fenders
crossing the Mojave."
Now she lifts them tenderly.
"They never seemed mine before."

4
A woman gave birth to a woman
who gave birth to me,
my nipples small and tight
on the jungle-gym of ribs,
mother's breasts filling her shirt
as she sweated the coastal incline,
grandmother strapping herself in gauze
to fit a flapper's gown,
until her breasts retreated
leaving only the mark of their tide.
It was before they clearcut
Tillamook Head, that mountain
eaten by white-toothed seas,
before the old-growth
cedar fell screaming
its awful bark-rip curse,
that embarrassed moment
when the headland
exhaled in grunting sighs.

The moss was so thick
our hands lost themselves
in the vagueness of rocks and logs.
We walked as if on pliant bodies
whose breath rose between our legs,
warm and humid and near.
Two mothers, two daughters,
the three of us hand
over hand up basalt,
easing down green deer slides,
through tunnels of time and age,
ambiguities of weather.
Three women turned inside out
in subtle, persistent motion,
crossing the mountain
between morning and evening,
from north to south.
At Ecola we emerged together
in sunlight, lizard-hot
bodies on angled cliff stone,
taking off our shirts to dry,
drinking from lichen-lipped falls.
From the bag I took peaches,
ripe and warm, pulling
the flesh into dripping chunks,
letting the thick juice run.

5
Talking to a woman, like eating,
sustains us in spite of our guilt.
As if the daylight gestures betray
dark messages, hunger and need.
There is a social anorexia
among these women, stripped clean
by life's expected betrayals,
biting their tongues in neat cafes
as if the taste of truth would catch,
lure them into indulgences

of affection and recognition,
fatten them past the reach of men
into each others arms.
Out the window I watch ripe pears
drop from her well-tended trees.
In everything she does not say
I hear my own confessions.

6
To the young nurse she babbles
of labor pains, green curtains
and the brilliant tropical fish
glimpsed in those demerol seas.
Always before she left the white walls
with more than she could hold,
the warm bundle on her breast,
the bags and baskets of fruit.
Is it really that she is diminished
or that these awkward visitors,
looking anywhere but at her body
newly smoothed into sheets,
have lost parts of themselves
calipers can't measure?
Her tongue is not bruised.
When she lifts her voice
from the avenues of sleep
it rings out like taxi horns,
shrill, demanding notice.
To her side she calls us,
friends, sisters, children,
holds us to her chest
until she cries with the pain
and we cry too, discovering
the same stubborn thrust of heart,
the same ecstasy of breath.

THE GARDENER

DENISE LEVERTOV

Very tall, very pale, a man of bone and mist, he moves up and down our street in all seasons, stopping now at one house now at another. It is Old Day, the gardener, and half the householders in the block employ him. The brick houses, connected by party walls, are all alike except that a few, at our end of the street, are wider by an additional room at the kitchen end, and thus have two entrances. All have front gardens, each with its familiar character—a dusty gloom of ground ivy or a blaze of flowers; and each flower garden specializes: some can be counted on for roses, some for dahlias. My mother's, in midsummer, is golden with California poppies. Here and there a laburnum or a red may tree leans out toward the passerby from behind the low iron railings that surround each front garden.

But behind every house is the far larger back garden, wholly invisible from the street, and only partly visible even to next-door neighbors (including those on the parallel street whose gardens are back-to-back with ours), for they are separated from one another with brick walls as tall as a grown person, and often a further privacy has been given to each by well-grown trees or lilac bushes planted along their three sides. If, from our own garden, I look down the line of back gardens, I see what seems to be a narrow forest. Standing on a wooden crate placed close to one of our side walls, I can look directly into Foxes' on the left, or I can move it over to see Cornwell's on the right; or, over the back wall, a bit of Burnes's garden and Mrs. Peach's (for those next-street houses are not exactly aligned with ours). Those four, then, are known. All other gardens, all the way down the street, are secrets. But Old Day knows every secret, must have seen even those in which he hasn't worked, and even what lies behind the houses on the far side of the street. He walks through the houses and out into the hidden squares. Do all have lawns? Do some have goldfish pools, shrubberies, arbors? In ours there is a rockery made of dark, porous, cindery stuff—tufa, perhaps. And the Cornwells have a rockery of smooth white rocks which, when Margaret Cornwell and I rub our hands on them, give off a magical silver dust.

Bone and mist, deliberate, sardonic in his silence, he tends and he destroys. My mother transplants some wild primroses from a distant hedgerow where she dug them up on a day in the country. She shows them to Old Day and firmly warns him against injuring them when he weeds the beds. He digs them up. This happens again, with other treasures. Each time she cries with disappointment and anger, swears she will not hire him again. But after a while he is back. He is capable of helping as well as of hindering.

One time a crew of Irishmen come to make a new lawn. My sister's Drama Society has rehearsed in the garden all summer and trampled the grass to death. So it is to be dug and turfed. The men carrying loads of new-cut slabs of turf pass back and forth from their horse and cart parked in the street, tramp through the kitchen gate, the front garden, the kitchen door, the kitchen, down a step into the scullery, out into the trellis-screened, paved utility yard, and into the garden. Kitchen and scullery smell of earth and new grass. The men shout to each other in a fine brogue. Old Day is there, watching, impassive. He has been told not to let them dig up my special daisy, one whose petals are tipped with red, which grows—wild, but cared for—at the corner of the grass plot, by the base of an iron post up which a climbing rose is trained, near the French windows of our drawing room. They have been told, he has been told; but they forget, and he watches and says not a word as a spade goes into that corner, cuts into the daisy's roots, turns the plant under into the soil.

The Cornwells, the Burnses, whose gardens are tidier than ours and less abundant, have fewer problems with him. It is the abundance of our garden, my mother's inclusive and generous style of horticulture, that he seems to punish. In my copy of *Parables from Nature* there is an engraving that shows Old Day. I have never read the story; most of the pictures in this book have, in fact, a life quite independent of the texts to which they are attached; but I can see well enough that he is a person of ancient power; indeed, an embodiment of Time—have I not heard the phrase, Old Father Time?—or of Death. In the engraving there are two representations of him: one shows him leaning forward to examine the inscription on a sundial; this figure wears a sort of sou'wester hat, and carries under his arm a telescope for looking into past and future. The sundial stands in a churchyard crowded with antique tombstones, leaning this way and that. In the lower right-hand part of the picture he is shown digging a grave. He's right down in the grave, shoveling out the dirt with the same spade he used to bury my mother's primroses. His white hair sticks out below the brim of his hat, and there's a pleasant smile on his face. "Active and Passive," is the caption beneath the engraving.

My mother claims Old Day is stupid as well as malevolent; but though she employed another gardener once, for a few months, in the end she took Day back. His imperturbable persistence is equivalent to reliability, and at least he wastes no time talking. And I, though he rarely says a word to me, and though I know he is a dark power, and though there is something alarming in the mild, complacent pleasantness of his expression as, in that dark engraving, he shovels out a deep hole for someone dead to lie in—I nevertheless have a secret liking for him.

I grow up, some houses are destroyed by bombs in the blitz, I'm away working as a hospital nurse, the war claims all the iron railings from the front gardens, the war ends, I marry and cross the ocean. Old Day asks after me. My mother is amazed.

Years later, our house long since bought by strangers, I revisit the street, note what has changed, what is unchanged, nod to the sinister laurel bush near our kitchen window. A long-ago neighbor tells me Old Day must have died, she thinks. "Yes," I say, "he was white-haired when I was a young child, and seemed even then like a walking skeleton; yes, I suppose he can't still be alive." But I know better. Bone and mist, pale, white-haired, grey-eyed, very tall, clothed in colors of ash and earth, a capricious demigod, he still moves in a stately shamble up and down the block, glides unobserved right through certain houses, brings life and blossom, death and burial to the rectangular sanctums closed off from each other by walls of brick and thickets of may, laburnum, apple trees, memory, time. He carries sometimes a spade, sometimes a scythe, and listens in silence to orders he will not obey. He has his own intentions.

FIVE POEMS

DEIRDRA BALDWIN

SUDDEN CHILL

I once moved walls with the imagination
    and drew back the shutters of windows where white
houses froze on the lawn that licks
    through the ears of ghosts.
I unfrenzied the baffle of birds
    and wove the light between the lattice staves.
    Crossed the moat with the low tide in my palms.
The unknown made room for me then
    and of all its houses, open doors.

But I was less the stranger then than now,
    "hurried down the hallway
    bell in hand to make harmony"
and no one standing in the center of all creation
    could mistake what tears the wing from the wall.

This morning I woke to a room
    larger than sleep had whispered pale
and though I was rested
    a nugget of sleep took firm in thought.

I could never unwind the geography that breaks from the wilderness.

What a marvel the sea coast is drained of its color
    and the dull batter of stones and shells under the pale sun.

I had never wanted to grow down
    past the contentment of misunderstanding—
my stippled orders lunge at the way of things

and I can see what is real now.
The broken jewel scattered to stud the bit of truth
    and catch the eye
        from "home in the root" to that mind.

The high feather bone and cloud caught.

INTERESTING TIMES

Her limbs have been fed with dogwood blossoms and though
time shakes things whole, every once in a while you can see the
detail show wide. Or hear the drop in the pool kissed by an old letter
or company past. Last night I heard an ancient Chinese curse—
May you live in interesting times. And eager for approval in the
home of a friend, stepped down from the hearth onto the tail of a cat.
Once in a dark room I watched the rush of water over the stones
skid at her eye for mention of certain words that sank to the bone.
And was not surprised. For three days the wind has been impossible
to break down in the mind and the air and trees have battered my
sleep and waked me while the dream was still ripening in the
morning. If I would study her motives, what could I learn that
would not be true of the card that is laid across or the three coins?
If I searched the whorl of the leaf node would her face not appear
baring the same signs? Still the many-legged story I heard scuttles
across the floor. The teller of that tale was wrong to point out the stars
and mark their resemblance aloud. Because even though her words
failed, I have been left the door open to doubt. Events better
forgotten trail out and the shape of my room continues to shift the
window of her house. Though her tears once fell beyond my need

to understand, I feed them to the dark corner now. Where the
blind spark flames and the children are caught sinking their fingers
into walls. If we talk on this matter, the shells will spill down their
tongues and inch back to the sea. If I would touch this bright burn,
how could I reconcile her pain? Reason gathers to me, but my
spirit drifts far from the home I would make strong and tangles my
weary hands. If no one had told me I could have forgotten the
tear that slits the pulse.

THE SPILL

The deep shadow spilled from the house, and the late-fallen sun
brings old troubles down. And drains color from the field. Though
years have braided gold the dark lines that travel the bark and slice
their path through the blanket of grasses. Every season I look out
and see there has been no return, how the month swims to the
window and stares. The dream that turned the corners of light and
dark slope no longer meet the harmony I spoke with myself then,
and the questions I once settled, like strangers balancing drinks on
the white lawn, have undone their coats and taken new eyes. If I
had known the common understanding rather than doubt, I
would have been spared the rush to blood. But it hardly seems
possible now to have boarded that wisdom in this house. If he had
hurried through one hundred winters he would never have reached
me in time. And the weight that charred my bones rides my heart like
a death star. If time could bathe my hands, I might forgive the knife
he took to the nets of mind. If the sky were suddenly pocked and the
fields blighted I would see no more lacking than with the small
mirror he chose to burden time. If I could break the fingers that grip
the ridge and drop them forever, I would pick up the stone and
bash that dark dream down. But my anger has no phantom to rip
from the heels of sleep. The pallor that presses cold to tip the blossom
open has shot through the limbs of the orchard trees. Already the
rags of fallen petals cluster the roots and the air appears too clear to
hold sun or its blue bowl. Or the wind that struggles on the leaf.

THOUGHT TRAIN

For Hannah Arendt

The train that carried me from this familiar place brought me no
comfort. Pinned to the smokehouse the arms and eyes of the past
battered the air and dropped the shape of the branch down to the
mass that stirred at my window. And filled my cup with poison and
borrowed my tongue. The rag of color that hung upon the bush
forgotten lost the one who last abandoned care and flew off with
doubt feathering after. The spill of odd structures clacked like teeth
and the language grew no link but the swollen rectangle risen like
a peacock and the simple mind of the dinosaur within, dreaming.
Each day the distance between there and here fed me the ration of
time. I was starved for the fox and the deer and the glint of fire
that inhabits the beetle and pulls him to the mouth of the leaf. For
the soft moonstone of the deer's eye and the star-shaped digger of
the mole. When I arrived they told me the master's house had
waned to a skull. And they suggested that I try myself against the
dust. The bowl of berries stank with mold. And the train continued
to climb the dark track. Through strange cities where no one could
name their hands without moaning. When I turned back I found
only this small patch of sky had fallen on my tongue. And my body
sunken in the dark of my eye begged to be allowed to come home.

THREESOME OVERLOOKING BLACK POOL

The General abandons himself to the woodwork as usual.
For him, the color of the wheel represents
a certain refinement, the flower fallen over the face
near his own, pleasant weight of circumstance.
A backwater of fierce trees, their greeny tips fresh
as the whitecaps of the first milkteeth. Abandons—

O polite tones and musical interstice of raven's wing!
Held. Helf like the eye in pigtail, like god's pull
at the servant's hank drawn through blue black heavens.

Abandons at the oblique infinite of will, his chair scrapes
and his chains rattle. Overhead the prick of early stars
flails at death. Into his hand, the insect he is floats.

I am the Thief who reads words inscribed upon a gold watch:
"To the General. With love from his cannibal heart."

In the next scene, the General rides with his striped horse,
and scratching the sea bedsore frees hormones of abandonment.

There is trouble finding the keys to unlock
the stiffened General where he is looped in birthing oil.

Only the rain promises—that sweet music with stuttering tongue—
to press or relent. As we deem it the General's justice
to be left alone. The General gets his justice.

Then—let us come upon the General, his carriage window open
and hooves thundering from his heart across all pain. Abandoned.

Abandoned. Abandoned. The kiss shot through hell remained.

Now—the curve of her foot and her lacks, they've mercy—
she has none. But orders the insects to the woodwork,
and dreams to the lad who once dreamed of being the General.
There in heaven's bud, the three are seated on a porch.
But one is god's heart, whose hand is always deep in the pocket.

FIVE POEMS

JOSEPH DONAHUE

ORPHANAGE

The children hold out their arms
and imitate airplanes.
They outrun August,
they cool in the sunlit rain.
To watch them, you might think
their abandonment
had ended.

A faint steam fills the street,
but you can still find home—
it's where the clouds move to
when they darken.

FOR JIM DRONEY

I was not prepared for the rain tonight
or the wind that drives it through clothes
or the handfull of incorrect change
as the impatient bus driver shuts the door

and leaves me parsing pennies on a curb
leaves me asking what in my life
have I ever been prepared for
except death and I'm not prepared for that,
only ready for it. Not that I don't make plans
but the plans I make are pillars of flame
that lead me into the desert leave me
to the discretion of scorpions leave me
to die with no habitat in sight
no angelic dwelling or even a pit
to chasten the remains.

In an off-orange house
on Nesmith Street a man I care for
almost died. The medicine that made
his blood thin worked too well. The seepage
into the brain by now has been corrected.
Wearied by therapy by the syncopation
of pills every two hours he greets me:
unworthy of his effort. I knew
for weeks how bad you were I did not
call or even send a fifty-cent gift shop card.

Though yours was the house to which I craved
admittance, trudging in snow and cold,
inarticulate, a high school dropout
from Christian Doctrine Class,
up a hill no car could climb.
What I would have said had I knocked I have
no idea. Too confused to make
an inappropriate social visit,
frozen in my tracks no less than now
as I try to tell you that you are
important to me, that lights in your house
seen through a light snowfall I can approach
no more readily than I can approach
any other thing I am dying in the cold
for lack of.

OFF SEASON

Relentless apparatus spirit
rock salt from the hold,
build a mountain against winter.
(The ship a rustbucket dead
in the water.)
                Conveyor belt
and crane rattle all night,
loading up municipal trucks
earmarked
                for half New England.
So much involved in burning
a road clear, so much thrives
on salt—

A couple thieve to and fro.
They lug a boxful back to their car
parked where the spillover spills
into a vacant lot.
All that is personal soon rots,
said Yeats, it must be packed
in either ice or salt.

One feels almost at home here
amid the homes nailed shut,
the padlocked arcades of childhood.
Portsmouth Mineral Co.—

Inside the wall around the dock
Atlantic grandeur reveals
its corrosive gist. Spotlit.
Waiting for the graveyard shift.

                One could heap
the entire rage of the dead
and get something like this—
a blasphemy, but useful.
Nothing in your past can match

this mountain,
           not the pittance
made shoveling out
the stranded on canceled
winter afternoons, not the plow
or the final orange salt-truck
grinding uphill—

Not the oblivion the storm
had been your guarantee of.
You were out free in the world
for a while, but now it's time
to go back, back amid those
whose tears these are.

PENANCE

The priest in his confessional hears lives
pass in error. He can only counsel
and absolve. He is only the instrument
of absolution. He can only pass in error
through the bleak lives of his parishioners
like a black wind down an idle street
or a breath through a broken instrument.
The priest in his confessional derives
the one sin which underlies the many.
He can only pass in terror judgment
upon the parishioner in the dark
who wants to be absolved of the life
he claims is an empty idle street
where he finds in his hands a broken instrument,
where he wanders like a sick black wind.
The priest in his confessional hears lives
pass in terror, which only his counsel
can absolve. The parishioner derives
a judgment from the bleak life of the priest

who has longed at times for death in the dark,
a black wind at the end of an idle street
who finds in his hands a broken instrument.

MARRIAGE

Of blessedness what remnant. A chalice
lofted in the celebrant's hand, recollected in hell.
The bride and the bridegroom are joined.
The sun above them on this blue afternoon
is a lofted chalice. For each of them
hell is recollection. For each of them
hell and blessedness are joined. Blue afternoon.
The father of the bride will not live long.
Already he is a remnant of what he was,
a chalice filled with recollection, lofted on
a blue afternoon. Of blessedness what remnant.
The bride and the bridegroom, the Eucharist
taken from the celebrant's hand, the blue
afternoon joined with a recollection of hell
where the ghost of the bride joins her father,
where a hand has set them in a sulphur chalice
hotter than the sun on a blue afternoon.
The desire of the bride will not live long,
a chalice she will drink dry. The bridegroom's hand
will place her in hell. For each of them hell
is the ghost of desire, the bread and wine
a remnant of what once was. The sun above them
lofted by an unseen celebrant, a blessedness
where hell was once believed to be.
The father of the bride will not live long.
Long enough to see his daughter's unhappiness,
long enough to pray the bridegroom burn in a hell
at the heart of the sun. On a blue afternoon
a chalice lofted in the celebrant's hand
sanctifies a marriage that will not live long.

Long enough for a child, a remnant who will
drink dry the chalice and cast it down,
cast down the Eucharist from the celebrant's hand.
Who will live long enough to see the gold robes
of the celebrant, the ghost of his grandfather,
as the bride and the bridegroom are joined,
are photographed, on a blue afternoon on
a church lawn, the chalice of the sun lofted
by an unseen blessedness, bright and distant
as hellfire to the saved.

PLAZA MAUÁ

CLARICE LISPECTOR

Translated from the Brazilian Portuguese by Alexis Levitin

The cabaret on Plaza Mauá was called The Erotica. And Luisa's stage name was Carla.

Carla was a dancer at The Erotica. She was married to Joaquim, who was killing himself working as a carpenter. And Carla "worked" at two jobs: dancing half nude and deceiving her husband.

Carla was beautiful. She had little teeth and a tiny waist. She was delicate throughout. She had scarcely any breasts, but she had well-shaped hips. She took an hour to make herself up: afterward, she seemed a porcelain doll. She was thirty, but looked much younger.

There were no children. Joaquim and she couldn't get together. He worked until ten at night. She began work at exactly ten. She slept all day long.

Carla was a lazy Luisa. When the time of night arrived for her to present herself to the public, she would begin to yawn, wishing she were in her nightgown in bed. This was also due to shyness. Incredible as it might seem, Carla was a timid Luisa. She stripped, yes, but the first moments of the dance, of voluptuous motion, were moments of shame. She only "warmed up" a few minutes later. Then she unfolded, she undulated, she gave all of herself. She was best at the samba. But a nice, romantic blues also turned her on.

She was asked to drink with the clients. She received a commission per bottle. She always chose the most expensive. And she pretended to drink: but hers wasn't alcohol. The idea was to get the clients drunk and make them spend. It was boring talking with them. They would caress her, passing their hands over her tiny breasts. And she in a scintillating bikini. Beautiful.

Once in a while she would sleep with a client. She would take the money, keep it well hidden in her bra, and the next day she would buy some new clothes. She had clothes without end. She bought blue jeans. And necklaces. A pile of necklaces. And bracelets, and rings.

Sometimes, just for variety's sake, she danced in blue jeans and without a bra, her breasts swinging among the flashing necklaces. She wore bangs, and, using a black pencil, painted on a beauty mark close to her delicate lips. It was adorable. She wore long pendant earrings, sometimes pearl, sometimes imitation gold.

In moments of unhappiness, she turned to Celsinho, a man who wasn't a man. They understood each other well. She told him her troubles, complained about Joaquim, complained about inflation. Celsinho, a successful transvestite, listened to it all and gave her advice. They weren't rivals. They each did their own thing.

Celsinho was the child of nobility. He had given up everything to follow his vocation. He didn't dance. But he did wear lipstick and false eyelashes. The sailors of Plaza Mauá loved him. And he played hard to get. He only gave in at the very end. And he only accepted dollars. He invested the money he got in exchange from the black market at the Banco Halles. He was very afraid of growing old and of being forsaken. Especially since an old transvestite is a sad thing. He took two envelopes of powdered vitamins a day for energy. He had large hips and, from taking so many hormones, he had acquired a facsimile of breasts. Celsinho's stage name was Moleirão.

Moleirão and Carla brought good money to the owner of The Erotica. The smoke-filled atmosphere, the smell of alcohol. And the dance floor. It was tough being forced to dance with a drunken sailor. But what could one do. Everyone has his métier.

Celsinho had adopted a little girl of four. He was a real mother to her. He slept very little in order to look after the girl. And there was nothing she didn't get: she got whatever was good, and always the best. Even a Portuguese nanny. On Sundays Celsinho took little Clare to the zoo at the Quinta de Boa Vista. And they both ate popcorn. And they fed the monkeys. Little Clare was afraid of the elephants. She asked: "Why do they have such big noses?"

Celsinho then told her a fantastic tale involving good fairies and bad fairies. Or else he would take her to the circus. And they would suck hard candies, the two of them. Celsinho wanted a brilliant future for little Clare: marriage with a man of fortune, children, jewels.

Carla had a Siamese cat who looked at her with hard blue eyes. But Carla scarcely had time to take care of the creature: either she was sleeping, or dancing, or out shopping. The cat was named Leléu. And it drank milk with its graceful little red tongue.

Joaquim hardly saw Luisa. He refused to call her Carla. Joaquim was fat and short, of Italian descent. It had been a Portuguese woman neighbor who had given him the name Joaquim. His name was Joaquim Fioriti. Fioriti? There was nothing flowerlike about him.

The maid who worked for Joaquim and Luisa was a cunning black woman who stole whatever she could. Luisa hardly ate, in order to keep her figure. Joaquim drowned himself in minestrone. The maid knew about everything, but kept her trap shut. It was her job to polish Carla's jewelry with Brasso and Silvo. When Joaquim was sleeping and Carla working, this maid, by the name of Silvinha, wore her mistress's jewelry. And she was kind of grayish-black in color.

This is how what happened happened.

Carla was confiding in Moleirão when she was asked to dance by a tall man with broad shoulders. Celsinho lusted after him. And he ate his heart out in envy. He was vindictive.

When the dance ended and Carla returned to sit down next to Moleirão he could hardly hold in his rage. And Carla, innocent. It wasn't her fault she was attractive. And, in fact, the big man appealed to her. She said to Celsinho:

"I'd go to bed with that one for free."

Celsinho said nothing. It was almost three in the morning. The Erotica was full of men and women. Many mothers of families went there for the fun of it and to earn a bit of pocket money.

Then Carla said:

"It's so good to dance with a real man."

Celsinho sprang:

"But you're not a real woman!"

"Me? How come I'm not?" said the startled girl, who, dressed that night in black, in a long dress with long sleeves, looked like a nun. She did this on purpose to excite those men who desired a pure woman.

"You," screamed Celsinho, "you are no woman at all! You don't even know how to break an egg! And I do! I do! I do!"

Carla turned into Luisa. White, confounded. She had been struck in her most intimate femininity. Confused, staring at Celsinho who had the face of a witch.

Carla didn't say a word. She stood up, crushed her cigarette in the ashtray, and, without saying anything to anyone, abandoning the party at its height, she left.

On foot, in black, on the Plaza Mauá at three in the morning. Like the lowest of whores. Alone. Without recourse. It was true: she didn't know how to fry an egg. And Celsinho was more of a woman than she.

The plaza was dark. And Luisa breathed deeply. She looked at the lampposts. The plaza was empty.

And in the sky, the stars.

SEVEN NEW ZEALAND POETS

ALISTAIR PATERSON · IAN WEDDE · RIEMKE ENSING
· DAVID MITCHELL · MICHAEL HARLOW · C. K. STEAD
· ALLEN CURNOW

Selected by Alistair Paterson

ALISTAIR PATERSON: TWO POEMS

BALLOON WATCHING

                          (*New Mexico, October, 1981*)

Balloons
        drift towards the mountains
the land moves under your feet
            the sea (already gone)
slides away from you:
you're here/
                  or not here
are somewhere else—
in a particular locality
                  where
all languages are one language
        all faces, one face . . .

It is "location"
   a part of the geography—
which means it's describable
      & therefore
comes under such headings/
labels/ designations:
    two mountains truncated
"forming notable features &
giving names to the place"
      pines (scattered)
& other vegetation
       . . . disorderly . . .

The problem
    is in the particulars:
Lawrence in New Mexico
       Frieda
strangers in a strange land
(a carnival of strangers)
       balloons
coloured, spectacular
drifting over the desert—
      over Santa Fe
& Chaco Canyon/ Taos
      the Rio Grande . . .

And the landscape
      burns in the sun—
is a haze of confusion
    (crushed, wrinkled)
an eroded parchment
with words written on it:
    a series of passage ways
(of passages)
interrupted, broken

                    —illuminated—
decorated by moths
                    butterflies . . .

FROM QU'APPELLE

Today
(which is the present—now)
she sings the sun—
                    & the sun's begetting
of a morning so bright
it reaches out catching the throat:
a supreme perfection of things
                    (particulars)
that have a handiness about them
                    that could be used.
She could make of this morning
a net or a boat—music—
                    a wooden bowl
something to fish with
or for travelling—
                    a scarf or a rug.
She sees that the sun is a climber
ascending the East   a journeyman
          who's mastered his trade
& knows how to use brush & ladder.
She is moved by it
                    waves to it
as if she knows that what's done well
is not done with ease
          & rarely for pleasure:
she recognises a wrestling
a striving
          a tension of opposites
                    morning

          & the sun rising.

IAN WEDDE: *FROM* GEORGICON

HEAVY BREATHING

A night in June   midwinter   harbour lights
melting under rain   "natural" as only you can be
when you're alone with the slow learner who loves you madly.
so tired and so happy   this ending which is a beginning
in which looniness isn't, you know? but confused desire
for clarity   thinking: night is a great shadow
sweeping across the world   behind it
zillions of beings are beginning to visit the dreams
(good line)
visit the dreams
which live in darkness   on the other side
zillions of others begin to visit the dreams that live
in light
       from which they get no rest
the work shoes dried hard near the hearth await your feet
the pets look at you with admiration   what a hunter
you are! capturing the meat in concrete
knowing when to go!
The refuse bucket fills up while the stockpot empties
what a rhythmical universe it is
                how like a dance
your waking and sleeping in the dreamy bunkhouse of love

SURVIVAL ARTS

When it's raining like this   ra   ining
& you're oiling your dreams with folly   oi   ling
the interior weather ruining the décor   rui   ning
doodling about with bits of paper
            and those moiré stains of disuse

under the skins of the weird Friday set
                           who take so long to go
        they decide they might as well stay
"a bit longer"   or for as long as it takes

                                As long as what takes? It doesn't matter
(That makes three "its")
         providing it's (IV) somebody else's idea
               stucco it (5) on to your personality
call in a garden consultant

Whoopee! now you are desirable
                              & you can go ahead & sell out

for a profit

When it's raining (ining ling ning) like this
in the drainpipe
trying to decant Friday's hangover
into Saturday's late velocity

                         Sometimes I think
I might as well talk to myself
             other times I know I'd be lost
without love's reviving punches to the heart
& all the tender decay you want to hold while there's time

TRI

What's to stop you
                being quiet this evening
long enough to think

about a child looking up at the
immensity of the universe of the
back yard   red-flowering trees beyond   (red)

                    beyond them the green sea   (green)
                                    dusky mountains
    purple (the sky)   (purple)
                        is that all? no:
                                        look:
                        a star/

                            & back here

    ants
    3 dimming quarter-moons
    for each triadic body:
                        the
    appetising smell
    of moist dirt:
                silver-buff structures of fallen *karo* leaves
    their brittle planes/

    What is there?   Oh it
    could be you
                or you
    or me
          worshipping thus with our play
    at such altars

                            That we see
                            without eyestrain

    The music
    of such
    common chords:
    we hear it, too
    & we are not deaf

GET LOST

I used to
Try again

>	I didn't
>	I wasn't
>	>	"used to"

anything/

Once

>	I liked

spring & autumn best:

>	That clarity out there

moving inside, perceptions
kissing detail:

>	>	Promise

at one end
>	>	at the other
"the goods."

Now ("at my age")

I'm in love with summer.

I'm beginning to trust joy

& that's hard, the space between
expectation & fulfilment
swarms with lost choices, you
"lose your way" like they
say, you
>	>	"get lost."

And doing it's
what I love now, losing myself
in it. Promise

has too many secrets, "the goods"
get more used each day

RIEMKE ENSING: A POEM

INHERITORS

To Amiria / 6th February, 1980

"They made our mother grow old"

you said, reading the diary
where the old lady spun her web
of words fragile as dawn on dew
in a valley where all sound is a twist
of wind as it curls
up the beach; the moan of trees holding
the earth up despite failure and generations
dead
scanning the pace of silence.

Amiria, *"of loving, several ways"*

These words you will know/will recognize
as days stretched beyond years
of remembering into history
we make
daily.

I see your mother in her garden also
the double cheerfulness that flowers

early, the smaller suns called daffodil.
Home a small place perched on a hill
looking out across islands. In winter
the polishing of gourds.
        But unusual
winds began to blow from over the harbour
where storms raged and shouted like children
riding a brawl wave/baring white teeth.
Rips and currents breaching in all directions.
The tumult, like curls of weed, fumed
on the beach, made ragged stone,
with too much bruising.

Bulbs were uplifted.
Journeys made
North.

Home then a small place curled in the lap
of the bay under the hill whose spine stood
straight in shafts of light at sunrise
protecting by distance and a sign saying

      leave your quarrels
      in the waters of this river
      as you enter the world of Taratara

also a peace flag flying

      leave your weapons
      on the edge
      as in Delphi weapons were

and everything sleep-eyed but wide awake
for the warm and cold side of the mountain
and the cleaned and scraped bones of ancestors
called back.

Was it McCahon who asked   "At the boundary
can I forbear from turning
my head?"

I rifle through histories and everywhere
people I recognize in you, landscapes,
and almost always, approaching clouds of pain.

On the flanks of Taratara
the ledger of ancestors sculpted
               in trees
                  waterfalls
                  rivers
                  the songs the birds make
                              when it rains
                  stones turned over
                      to talk
                          in the hand

and in everything   the calling
of names, the register of family
dispersed by whatever weather
to the corners of grief,
to come and give to the land
the korowai.

DAVID MITCHELL: A POEM

TH LESSON

it was
the attic messenger
came to me
in a dream . . .

his sandall'd feet
strode
      the blue air
above the holie
stream

&

all abt./

    his sirens
          were

as
  white birds
        on th green . . .

&

in his hand
there sprang a heart

to mark
what i must say

&

from that heart
there blew a rose

th slow winds bore
away . . .

&

on each petal
of that rose

th sleek worm lay
soft curl'd

&

in th book
of that quiet fire

i read
what delphi told
      th passing &
      th passing &
      th passing of
      a world.

MICHAEL HARLOW: TWO POEMS

THE DINNER PARTY

Words survive, just
behind the weeds
of conversation—
never do they clamour
for "banqueting delights"
sit large and gaudy
at assembly, or any other
intimacy we might
design:
    look, how they
dream in the crowns
of flowers, how they
pass the time (and time
again, so composed,
shining under
scarves of light
how they wait
in holes of quiet:
        there is
music to be heard
and to be
    heard

        now

"ELEMENTARY," MINUTE OBSERVATIONS

The intimate revelations
of pipes, watches, and bootlaces
are all his care the shaman,
detector Holmes—he is a man scanning
the horizon, say, for the dark
mark of a squall, or the healer's
true god, light
            Cigars in the
coal-scuttle, in the pointed toe
of a Persian slipper, exotic tobacco;
in his mouse-coloured dressing gown
he cultivates no less
than the "aesthetics of surprise":
those minute observations
of the heart that do not lie
when the world is wide to the eye,
the witness just ordinarily, wise.

C. K. STEAD: *FROM* TORONTO

THE TOWER

This is the world's tallest
                man-made
construction
          not to call it
"vulgar"
"pretentious"
        all our aspirings
are
        and men on plains
        like to build towers.

   Tonight there's a green
half-moon

               tucked in under
the revolving restaurant
 and I wish the tower began
there
               a flying saucer
up out over
the city skyline
          emitting light like
shafts of mechanical
song.

EAST OF NORTH

No need for this shaping
               search for "meaning"
(is it?)
       down there the street's
wet
               two spiked spires
and under the disco sign
fifteen floors down
       can see she's in rags
the woman
          going through garbage.

          Somewhere north there
east of north
the apartment walked from
               with Miroslav
                    Libby's
who kissed us both at the door
"Goodbye"
               the freckled nose
the voice like honey
a mouth not to be shared.

DARK

The gold building
                repeats the black
in broken reflection
                lake front lost
beyond freeway flyover
                            tower
hanging in there
                in mist the moon
                    flies from
floats through
                dust underfoot
                and paper
                and prayer
                close curtains
of this dark dream.

NIGHT CLUB

"Easy listening
criminals"
                the makers of
this nightclub
noise
                but we dance to it
                    how we dance
it's like our champagne bodies
croon to it
           duet of hair and hands and
                        moving to it
this honey
                    soft centered
            "cornball at the core"

like living again
                like loving.

FACES

Today
            Miroslav and I
         walking from Dundas
East to a bank on Queen
and Spadina.

Rained so / beating
                      bought
   umbrellas
            twelve dollars
                50 self
opening.

          My triggered spring
he liked
                yes but his
wasn't so flimsy.

                Waited
in a glass cage
     pelted by the flowers of
rain.

"I suppose it's you" (frowning:
the girl in the bank)

he too
     showing the passport face
of another man.

      Tonight his face takes off
            for Prague
              mine
for London.

          Passports go with them
and poems
                 these polite
concealing lines
          thanking Toronto
          wishing it well.

ALLEN CURNOW: A POEM

CANST THOU DRAW OUT LEVIATHAN WITH AN HOOK?

I
An old Green River knife had to be scraped
of blood rust, scales, the dulled edge scrubbed
with a stone to the decisive whisper of steel
on the lips of the wooden grip.

You now have a cloud in your hand
hung blue dark over the waves and edgewise
luminous, made fast by the two brass rivets
keeping body and blade together, leaving
the other thumb free for feeling
how the belly will be slit and the spine severed.

The big kahawai had to swim close
to the rocks which kicked at the waves
which kept on coming steeply steaming,
wave overhanging wave
in a strong to gale offshore wind.

The rocks kicked angrily, the rocks
hurt only themselves, the seas without a scratch
made out to be storming and shattering,
but it was all an act that they ever broke
into breakers or even secretively

raged like the rocks, the wreckage of the land,
the vertigo, the self-lacerating
hurt of the land.
                    Swimming closer
the kahawai drew down the steely cloud
and the lure, the line you cast
from cathedral rock, the thoughtful death
whispering to the thoughtless,

Will you be caught?

II
Never let them die of the air,
pick up your knife and drive it
through the gills with a twist,
let the blood run fast,
quick bleeding makes best eating.

III
An insult in the form of an apology
is the human answer to the inhuman
which rears up green roars down white,
and to the fish which is fearless:

if anyone knows a better it is a man
willing to abstain from his next breath,
who will not be found fishing from these rocks
but likeliest fished from the rip,

white belly to wetsuit black, swung copular
under the winching chopper's bubble,
too late for vomiting salt but fluent at last
in the languages of the sea.

IV
A rockpool catches the blood,
so that in a red cloud of itself
the kahawai lies white belly uppermost.

Scales will glue themselves to the rusting blade
of a cloud hand-uppermost in the rockpool.

V
Fingers and gobstick fail,
the hook's fast in the gullet,
the barb's behind the root
of the tongue and the tight
fibre is tearing the mouth
and you're caught, mate, you're caught,
the harder you pull it
the worse it hurts, and it makes
no sense whatever in the air
or the seas or the rocks
how you kick or cry, or sleeplessly
dream as you drown.

A big one! a big one!

NOTES
ALISTAIR PATERSON, who is currently employed in Auckland as a member of the New Zealand Education Department's tertiary inspectorate, has published four books of poetry, an anthology of New Zealand poetry, and a short critical work. He is currently editor of the literary journal *Pilgrims* and writes art and other critical articles. In 1976 he initiated and organized the visit of Robert Creeley to New Zealand.

IAN WEDDE lives in Wellington. His most notable books are *Earthly, Sonnets for Carlos* (1976), and *Dick Seddon's Great Dive,* a novel which won a New Zealand Book Award in 1977. His most recent publication is a collection of poems, *Castaly* (1981). He is recognized as being the leading and most gifted of younger New Zealand poets and prose writers.

RIEMKE ENSING teaches English at Auckland University. She has edited an anthology, *Private Gardens,* and recently published her first collection, *Letters,* from which "Inheritors" has been taken.

DAVID MITCHELL, who has published one collection, *Pipe Dreams in Ponsonby,* has been a Katherine Mansfield Fellow in Menton, France, and currently conducts regular Tuesday-night readings at the Globe Tavern in Auckland. He has a second book in preparation.

MICHAEL HARLOW, who teaches at Canterbury University, has published several selections of his work. His latest book, *Today Is the Piano's Birthday,* was issued in 1982.

C. K. STEAD is a professor of English at Auckland University. He has an international reputation as a poet, novelist, short-story writer, critic, and editor. One of his works, *Smith's Dream,* has been produced as a full-length feature film. In 1981 he held a research fellowship and completed a major critical study of twentieth-century poetry.

ALLEN CURNOW, who has been writing longer than any other New Zealand poet, is a former university teacher. Anthologist, playwright, critic, and poet, he epitomizes the professional approach to poetry. In 1981 he won a New Zealand Book Award for his *An Incorrigible Music,* from which his contribution has been taken. The permission of Auckland University Press and the author is acknowledged.

DR. ARNOLD BIEDERMEIER'S SUICIDE PARLORS

a way out of the ordinary

URSULE MOLINARO

It was in aesthetic self-defense that Dr. Arnold Biedermeier first conceived of suicide parlors: He was growing ear-shaped. At least the top half of him was growing ear-shaped.

He noticed it late one winter afternoon as he was leaving his office. When he happened to look at himself leaving his office —in his raccoon coat & matching hat— in the wall-wide mirror he'd installed to the left of his desk, for patients to face themselves while they sat talking about themselves.

His patients rarely faced themselves. They'd have little need of him if they could face themselves. Their self-preoccupations were verbal rather than visual, at least for the 40 minutes they spent sitting across from him, murmuring/muttering/hissing/occasionally yelling their injured monologues.

The cumulative effect of which was beginning to deform his initially well-proportioned —& subsequently weight-controlled— torso.

He could see it clearly in the mirror —delaying his departure from the office by 40 minutes; after removing his coat—: the lengthening lobe of his stomach. The pinkish furl at the tip of his head. With a few illuminated hairs bristling around the shell. His initially well-boned face was caving into a canal, furrowed by years of listening to his patients' polyphonous complaints. & self-justifications.

Justified complaints, many times, about circumstances truly beyond their control. Unbearable circumstances which they kept attracting, & begged him to take away. To make bearable with the rainbow-colored pacifiers he held out to them, with scientific father fingers.

With Big Brother fingers, to younger male patients. Who often rejected his pacifiers. & his fingers. Demanding the real stuff. To stop the pain of living. To stop it all. Once & for all. Instead of anesthetized more-of-the-same tomorrows. Wishing that they were dead.

Before leaving his office that falling winter night, Dr. Biedermeier phoned an old friend, & asked her to meet him for dinner.

During dinner, he pushed his chair away from the table, & asked the old friend to take a close look: Did she notice anything out of the ordinary, something different, looking at him from the top down to where the table cut across his crossed knees.

The old friend wanted to know what it was she was supposed to notice: New jeans? . . . It was hard to tell with him: He was always wearing the same   tight   uniform of the nonconformist. The knobby white sweater certainly wasn't new: She'd given it to him for Christmas a year ago . . . Did he want her to notice that he was wearing it? . . . Ah! He had once again splurged on new frames for his glasses . . .

Dr. Biedermeier heaved a patient sigh & petulantly informed her that he was turning into an ear. At least the top half of him was turning into an ear. Couldn't she see it?

She couldn't. To her, Arnold Biedermeier was & always had been mainly a mouth.

He walked out on her over brandies, almost tempted to leave her with the check. He'd made a mistake, expecting a woman   —even a professionally sensitive woman: a successful photographer of theater faces—   to notice changes in a man's body. Few women looked at men as bodies. They mainly looked at men's social positions. It didn't seem to matter if the positions had unaesthetic torsos; & tweedy erections.

But he'd been afraid to go to his bar & expose a nascent ear to the sensitive eyes of the young men he met there. Who'd ignore him   or worse: might start reacting to him like women: to the affluent doctor rather than to: Arnie, who was practically one of their own cruisable selves; only slightly older; & richer   if they saw what he had seen in his office mirror.

Which he saw again   unmistakably   in his bathroom mirror when he got home from dinner. & again unmistakably the next morning, while carefully shaving along the upper curve of the external auditory canal. & again at 11 a.m., back in his office. When he sat down in his patients' chair, in an honest effort to face himself squarely.
 Or rather: convexly & concavely. Not sure what color pacifier to hold out to the momentous ear he saw sitting across from him, above a pair of tight-jeaned legs, & ankle-booted feet. Anxiously peering through tinted Christian Dior glasses.
 Framed in genuine-tortoise thoughts of suicide.

Which was readily accessible to him. Without pain, or bungling.
 Unlike his patients, he had legal access to the real stuff, to end it all once & for all, if he so chose. If he chose not to face more-&-more-ear-shaped tomorrows.

At this point, facing himself in all honesty, concavely & convexly in his office mirror, he was struck by the enormity of his selfishness.
 & of his professional incompetence: pacifying symptoms, but rarely able to remove the causes of his patients' complaints.
 His humbled mind drew a blank. & was graced with a revelation. A timid smile dimpled the ear canal, as though God's little finger had suddenly loosened an obtuse bit of wax: Suicide needed to be made accessible to all of suffering humanity. Not only to doctors & dealers.
 If people were offered a place where they could go to die in peace, painlessly   perhaps even pleasurably   24 hours a day, 7 days a week, year-round, including holidays   —especially the suicidal holidays, such as Thanksgiving & Christmas—   they would be alive by their daily choice. & would have to stop complaining.
 & he would be able to recover his former shape. A desirable shape, even by the sensitive standards of young men in bars, considering that he was 42.

Dr. Arnold Biedermeier acted on his revelation. He got on the phone & canceled his appointments for the day. Then he composed a concise proposal for the setting up of an experimental suicide parlor in New York City   to be followed by a chain of gvt.- or state-supported suicide parlors throughout the nation, if not the world, & mailed it to a former   dead   patient's husband, whose prominent public face he had saved from rumors of foul play, a number of years ago, by testifying to the dead patient's recurrent suicide attempts.

Perhaps the   promptly remarried   widower would use his incontrovertible public weight to encourage the establishment of suicide parlors as one of the human services of the Department of Health & Human Services.

Dr. Biedermeier wrote eloquently about the right to self-destruction, as one of the true criteria of individual freedom in a civilized society. Instead of that society's insistence that indivduals preserve themselves for unsolicited collective annihilation.

About freedom of choice, building individual responsibility for being, by being offered the choice not to be.

About quality of life as opposed to unimaginative suffering.

About the moral   & economic   questionability of enforced prolongation of painful, often unendurable existences.

For which his suicide parlors would offer not only a humanitarian solution, but a compensation. Something to look forward to: a personalized death, wish-designed to accommodate every conceivable ego image & fantasy.

Under the compassionate supervision of competent psychiatrists. With the aid of competent anesthetists, nurses, secretaries, masseurs, priests (of all denominations), philosophers, storytellers, theater directors, musicians, visual artists, jugglers, caterers, flowershops; & funeral parlors.

Life-weary individuals could come & let themselves be put to sleep painlessly. In peaceful privacy, holding an understanding hand. Or during a banquet, in the company of friends. Watching or enacting a play. Or listening to music.

—Dictating their memoirs . . . Provided the dictation did not exceed 24 hours: the death-wish-indulgence limit allowed each registered applicant. During which time span applicants were also allowed to change their minds.

There were no other restrictions. Life-weary individuals could come & poison/cut/stab/shoot/hang/ax/drown/club/stone/burn/freeze themselves to death, with expert counsel & assistance. The parlor supplied all necessary tools & equipment.

If the gvt. took advantage of his proposal, & allotted the funds necessary for its nationwide realization, these multiple services could be made available free of charge to every suffering individual, & yet be to the gvt.'s earlier-mentioned economic advantage.

Especially in view of the recent upsurge of age gangs, composed of hollow-eyed senior citizens who had taken to the streets of the larger cities since the discontinuation of their social security checks. & were not only obstructing traffic with their arthritic panhandling & shrill-feathered outdoor sleeping arrangements, but were also a demoralizing sight for taxpayers on their way to work.

He trusted that his former patient's widower was still gratefully remarried . . . & looked forward . . . to . . . etc. . . .

Dr. Arnold Biedermeier's eloquent proposal did not fall on deaf ears.   —Deafness might have been another alternative; but a selfish one.— However, the gvt. saw little reason for pampering refugees from life with a lavish death.

Which would, moreover, be wasted on the age gangs, which were composed of persons mostly beyond the age of sensory refinements. Their threat   though real enough with regard to traffic, & regrettably demoralizing   might perhaps be countered with more expedient, collective, egalitarian means.

Unfortunately one of the most expedient means had been regrettably discredited by a historical precedent, & rather than having recourse to it at this point in time, the gvt. deemed it wiser to let nature take its course. A roofless, food-scarce existence on winter city streets could not be overly conducive to longevity.

However: the gvt. would not stand in the reputed doctor's way, if he wished to try his experiment on his own & set up an initial suicide parlor in New York City. Preferably a less ambitious one, that would allow for an eventual emphasis on the aforesaid less individualized, egalitarian democratic expediency. With best wishes . . . etc. . . .

There was a check, signed by his former patient's obviously still grateful widower. A personal loan, convertible into an initial investment in the establishment of eventual, gvt.-supported chains of suicide parlors, if the first one caught on.

The check was large enough to acquire a burned-out building in a questionable neighborhood. To redesign the interior, & equip it with flexible facilities to accommodate the fantasies of 24 individuals during one 24-hour period. & to pay a modest salary to a small but dedicated staff. Of one: Dr. Arnold Biedermeier.
Who felt that he was answering a crying need.
But death   especially voluntary death   had been so successfully discredited in this complaining, blaming society that despite eloquent ads, & pep talks to the most miserable of his patients, only 3 candidates presented themselves on opening day. None of whom he knew. 2 bums, & 1 bag lady.

The first bum looked 80, but insisted that he was 42, the same age as Dr. Biedermeier. When asked by what means he wished to die, he demanded a single room, & enough Bourbon to drink himself to death.

Although this demand exceeded the 24-hour-death-wish indulgence limit, Dr. Biedermeier acquiesced. He was eager to get his project under way.

The second bum was in his late twenties, somewhat unkempt & emaciated, but still plausible as a body. He said that he used to be a writer, forced to earn his living as a proofreader for a textbook publisher. Who had fired him for inserting pertinent facts about Jefferson's sex life into a high-school history book. Since then he had been living by his wits, on a diet of coke & grass.

His wish was to die at the end of a meditation. To enter cosmic consciousness during a mescaline high, & then be finalized with a painless, imperceptible needle.

The bag lady, who refused to give her age, wanted to die like Cleopatra, with 2 vipers at her breast   (symbolizing her 2 daughters). After a bubble bath, a wash & set, a manicure, a pedicure, a steak dinner with wine, & a good night's sleep naked between satin sheets.

The next morning the old bum & the bag lady said they'd changed their minds about wishing to call it quits just yet, & stumbled out into the street like kids released from school, laughing & shoving each other.

Dr. Biedermeier was left with the young proofreader's still plausible, spaced-out body —which would not have looked out of place in his bar— propped against a wall in the lotus position. With vacant, pale-blue eyes.

With a sigh he sat down beside the body, & slowly crossed his legs. Which wasn't easy, in skin-tight jeans. He had brought 2 syringes, filled with the real stuff, precision-dosed according to body weight: 126 & 162 lbs. respectively.

He felt that his suicide parlor was everything he had promised: permitting an ear to die in the company of blue-eyed silence.

TWO POEMS

ERNESTO CARDENAL

Translated from the Spanish by Jonathan Cohen

RALEIGH

Due east from Peru, towards the sea, by the Equinoctial line,
upon a white lake of salt water 200 leagues long
lies Manoa,
Manoa, mansion of the sun, mirror of the moon,
Manoa that Juan Martín had seen one day
when at noon as he entered it they removed his blindfold
and he traveled all that day till night through the city.
I knew about it for years from reports
how it glimmers at night on the moony lake
and the splendor of the gold at noon.
All the vessels of his house, table, and kitchen, were of gold
says Gomara
and they found 52,000 marks of good silver, and 1,326,500
pesos of gold,
he says about the treasure of Atahualpa in Cuzco,
that they found 52,000 marks of good silver
and 1,326,500 pesos of gold.
For they said that the stones we brought were not gold!
And I spoke with the caciques in their houses
and gave wine to the Spaniards in Trinidad to get them talking.

And I learned about all the rivers and kingdoms;
from the East Sea to the borders of Peru,
from the Orinoco southward as far as the Amazon
and the region of María Tamball,
all the kingdoms.
And the way of life that's followed in them, and their customs.
Orenqueponi, Taparimaca, Winicapora.
It was as if I were seeing them.
The Indians along the shores, those on the islands, the Cannibals,
Cannibals of Guanipa,
the Indians called Assawai, Coaca, Aiai,
the Tuitas dwelling on trees, the Headless Ones
and the Wikiri north of the Orinoco
and the Arwaca south of the mouth of the Orinoco
and beyond them, the Cannibals
and south of them, the Amazons.
And so we set out in April
when queens of the Amazons gather at the borders
and dance naked, anointed with balsam and gold,
till the finish of that moon—
We set out in April
our ships quite a long way from us anchored at sea,
on the venture—
100 men with their bags and their supplies for a month
sleeping out in the rain
and bad weather and in the open air and in the burning sun
and plants getting stuck to their skin and the wet clothes
and the sweat of so many men together and the sun's heat—
(and I who remembered the Court)
and a sadness growing heavier by late afternoon and the buzzing
    from the swamps
and we'd hear monkeys at night crying filled with fear,
the scream of an animal frightened by another
and the noise of some oars,
the plash of some leaves in the river,
the step of gentle hooves upon leaves.
Voices: the sadness of those voices . . .
No prison so lonely exists in England.

And already very little bread. And not a drop of water.

Nights in cots hanging under the sky of Brazil—
that kind of bed they call "hamacas"—
hearing the current rushing in the darkness
and the drum from tribe to tribe up in the mountains
and the roar of water growing louder.

No bread. No water.
Our ears dazed by silence.
The trees so high we couldn't feel the air.
And the roar of water growing louder.

No bread. No water.
Except for the murky water of the river, that's all.
And there's a red river that turns poisonous when the sun sets
and while the sun is down one hears it groan, and get sick.
And some lagoons black and thick, like tar . . .
And the heat as we drew toward the Line.
And the smell of wet leaves and the taste of weariness.
And from rapids to rapids, from cascade to cascade,
the laughter at nightfall of the green virgin of the river
and the crashing of water into water.

And the air weakening. And the jungle lonely . . .

My company beginning to lose hope.
And a day short of the land where all one desires is found!
And on the banks, flowers and ripe green fruits.
And some green birds—
we amused ourselves a good while watching them pass—
And breadfruits and monkeys and the Campana bird
and the sweet fragrance of balsam and soapberry
and the wax that the Karamana tree secretes
and the moisture in those jungles of sandalwood and camphor:
the trees were abounding in milk and honey,
they were abounding in amber and fragrant gums—
and some fruit that would burst with a bang—
from afar we'd hear it at night exploding.

And leaves big as canoes would fall upon the river.
And we saw the Crystal Mountain, we saw it afar off,
standing on the horizon like a silver church
and a river fell from its top with a terrible noise like
    a thousand bells.
And the daughters of the Orinoc laughing amid the trees . . .
And cascades that shone from afar like cities,
like a smoke rising over some great town
and the rumble and thunder and rebounding of the waters.
I never saw a more beautiful country:
the virgin green valleys,
the birds toward the evening singing on every tree,
the stags that came tamely to the water as to a master's whistle
and the air fresh with a gentle easterly wind
and golden stones glittering in the sunlight.

Fifteen days later we sighted Guiana, to our great joy,
and a strong push of northerly wind blew that afternoon
and by night we reached a place where the river opens into
    three branches
and that night we lay at anchor under the stars, smelling
    the fragrance of Guiana.
The nearness of the land of Guiana!
But we had to head back eastward
because the rains began: those great downpours
and the rivers flooded, and endless swamps—
leaving behind Guiana with its sword of fire,
leaving Guiana to the sun, whom they worship.
And we entered the sea once more, all very sad . . .

STAR FOUND DEAD ON PARK AVENUE

The bolts of lightning woke me up
like the noise of furniture being moved and rolled across a floor
    upstairs
and later like millions of radios

or subway trains
or bombers
and it seemed that all the thunderbolts in the world
were hitting the lightning rods of skyscrapers in New York
and they stretched from the Cathedral of St. John the Divine to
    the Times Building
        Speak not to us, Lord. Speak not to us lest we die
from the Woolworth Tower to the Chrysler Building
and the flashes were lighting up the skyscrapers like photographers
        Let Moses speak to us.
        Speak not to us, Lord, lest we die
"He probably died last night around 3 a.m."
the New York Times later said.
I was awake then. The lightning woke me up.
The sky made starry by apartments and bathrooms
the lights of lawful and illicit love affairs
and of people praying, or robbing a safe right upstairs
or raping a girl as a radio plays full blast
or masturbating, or not being able to sleep
and people getting undressed (and drawing their curtains)
And the noise from the 3rd Avenue El
and the trains that come out of the ground at 125th Street
and go back down again,
a bus stopping and starting up at a corner
(in the rain), the scream, perhaps, of a woman in the park,
and the wailing of ambulances in the empty streets
or the red fire engines for all we know speeding to our own address
". . . His body was found by Max Hilton, the artist,
who told police he found him on the bathroom floor,
the floor's pattern pressed into his wet cheek
and he was still clutching a vial of white pills in his hand,
and in the bedroom a radio was playing full blast
just picking up static."

THE COSMETIC FACTORY

RUSSELL HALEY

The chimney stack in this reconstructed room has been completely exposed by the removal of the tongue-and-groove kauri lining. The bricks of the stack are yellow and have been sandblasted. Their color is so soft and delicate from this treatment that they appear warm, almost penetrable to the touch, even without a log fire burning in the grate. The stack rises to the wooden ceiling in steps. It looks like a machine with no moving parts. Some of those in the room say it resembles a pyramid. If the ceiling and roof were removed it might be possible to plot the movements of the planets. Mercury is certainly visible at this time of the year.

In the narrow area of ceiling between the chimney stack and the load-bearing exterior wall of the house there is set a loft panel which gives access to the attic.

Suddenly he remembers that his father visited Germany in 1936 though he did not attend the Olympics.

If he climbed the chimney by the stepped formation he could push his head against the loft panel. It would lift. His shoulders might just fit the gap.

The guests have assembled in this house to listen to a talk on the art of making films. There is no doubt that it will be an illustrated presentation.

A woman leans forward and touches the fringe of his hair.

'You have a gray streak. Is it natural or did you dye it?' The sun has shone all day but now it is evening. Outside it is pitch dark.

"I remember war being declared," he said. "On the wireless."

And if you turned your head in that narrow space would you see a flat landscape extending for twenty-five miles through three hundred and sixty degrees? A green landscape which might pass, at first glance, for Holland or Belgium. Or would your gaze light on a corner of a secret room where items were hoarded against the possibility of another disaster? Electronic consumer goods, quilts, canned goods, boxes of cosmetics.

He was quite aware as he drove here this evening that the name of the suburb bothered him. Not only that. He had lived in this city most of his life and yet had never visited this district. There was a park which he entered by a wide stone arch. Then volcanic slopes with the bulk of the mountain on his right. And he gained the distinct impression, even in the dim streetlights, that the houses obeyed some overall architectural plan. So definite was this notion that he had imagined he could park his car in any blind street and a door would open, light spill out, and he might enter, nod to an elderly man sitting in a carved chair, and then make his way through corridors and private rooms to this very place with the pyramidal stack.

Instead, he had followed the map printed on the invitation. Had parked his car in a street which shimmered with the heat from used vehicles.

In the right of way, as he approached, a couple in elegant clothing had been embracing under the dark mantle of a tree. Their moving feet had crushed small yellow fruit into the paved ground.

His host has employed a barman for this event. On examination he appears to be far too old for the task for which he has been hired. His scanty hair is combed sideways. There is not a streak of color left in it though it does not have the purity of white hair. It is like dirty snow. But he wears a drab-olive uniform with military insignia.

"I'd like a glass of white wine."

The barman replies in a foreign tongue which is immediately comprehended. They smile at each other. The glass is filled. He feels no terror.

When he answers it is in the same language. Such facility has been made possible by the vision of the room above the ceiling.

One thing he would like to do is to sort out the black-market goods into ordered piles so that he could select the items he required for his trip into Germany. His father in 1936 took an inferior English camera and regretted his mistake. It meant that he could not return with a Voigtlander or a Leica.

He will not make the same errors. His shoulders will fit the gap. He will force his way into that interior.

"Time for the preview!" The host leads his guests into a large bedroom where he has set up a screen and projector. As the lights are dimmed images immediately appear.

A roll of barbed-wire uncoils on a field of paper fragments. Some of the barbs pierce individual bits of white paper. Four characters dressed in black take each corner of the oblong section of wire and flip it over. A hand reaches across the lens and selects one piece of paper. The hand now appears to be detached from the black arm. The paper is held up close to the camera. A name—Hans Kreffeld—is typed on the paper.

One of the guests in the darkened room begins to cough. In spite of this he lights another cigarette. Smoke billows across the screen as the name fades.

Hans waits to see no more. He moves back into the room with the exposed chimney and begins to climb. He pushes up his gray-streaked head into darkness. His shoulders touch against something firm yet slightly yielding—it feels like clay rather than timber. And light from an unknown source rises.

Hans chooses the skis and ignores the electronic equipment. The way into Germany is clear and simple. As the truck grinds its way up the steep gradient in snow it is an easy matter to grasp the chain dangling from the tailboard. Hans is towed slowly into Germany as though on a ski-lift.

In the surveillance room of the cosmetic factory Hans is made to empty his pockets. The guard hands him a key to a locker and he suggests, in German, that Hans should place his personal possessions inside the locker, close the door firmly, and retain the key. Hans understands almost before the words are spoken. He is allowed to keep a small notebook and a fountain pen although the guard unscrews the barrel of the pen and inspects the little rubber tube inside. In fact he squeezes out one blot of ink on to a clean sheet of paper and sniffs at the drop.

"Germany and your country were once enemies," he says. "But all is forgiven now, is it not so?"

Hans had momentary difficulties with the structure of the language. Is it not so? It is. Not. So. Yes. Forgiven but not forgotten. His own father had been interned during the war. In his adopted country. An immigrant with a name like that! His journey home had been viewed with suspicion.

Hans received his pen and his visitor's pass. He was advised to pin the latter to his lapel.

"You'll find every nationality represented here," the guard said. "Just like the Olympics. And they will all understand that you are a distinguished person if you keep your pass visible." He saluted with a curiously sly smile and turned away.

Hans takes sweet tea in a small café where money is refused. As he drinks slowly he leafs through a copy of *Vogue* which has been left on the table. Every advertisement is for the products of the German cosmetic factory although the brand names might suggest that the beauty aids originated in France or Japan. All the female models have their eyes closed as though to emphasize better the detail and color of eye shadow, liner, rouge, powder, body tint, hair dye. Hans blinks and touches his face nervously. Flesh tone fills the darker lines and whorls of his fingerprints: "I've been made up," Hans murmurs to himself.

A young man at a nearby table laughs suddenly. The roots of his teeth are stained black from the thick sticks of liquorice he has been eating.

The young man is a Turk. His father worked as a porter in the streets of the Sirkeli district of Istanbul. He does not spend any time devising means of getting into Turkey. Kemer can remember the weight of his father's leather pack-harness and of how the old man walked in a permanent crouch even on his day off work.

Hans is joined by Kemer at his table where Hans is now finishing his tea. They each discuss who they are in a mutual language. Hans tells Kemer of the volcanic hills of his home city. Even in the closely plotted suburbs where houses run up the volcanic slopes there are observable temperature changes within the nearly extinct hearts of the mounds. Fumaroles might suddenly appear beneath a garden shed or glasshouse. Hot air, steam, lava, or even an earthquake were all still remotely possible.

Kemer tells Hans about the Blue Mosque—the vast leather doors which retain the image of a nomadic tent—and where sudden religious conversions had been known to happen.

The uniformed guard reaches in across their table. Hans and Kemer look at the fingernails. The guard is making spiders with his hands. The nails are clubbed with a purple tinge. This coloration is not from nail varnish but from natural causes. The guard has a heart problem.

The right hand moves. It crawls across the table toward Hans.

"You—going on your tour." The left hand moves elaborate legs. "And you—working, working."

Kemer stands up, backs away, turns, and walks. Very soon he is out of sight—slipping away between display partitions outside the café door.

"Mr. Kreffeld commences that way." The guard points. His finger trembles. "Your pass is your privilege. There are sections where even the workers are not allowed."

Hans starts to walk away down a narrow corridor.

"Turkey and your country were once enemies," the guard calls. It is the last time that Hans sees or hears him.

Steel doors draw back heavily into concrete walls as Hans cuts a photoelectric beam. He understands that he has entered the Eastern Zone where processes and products must be regarded as confidential.

On his left there is a rank of display cabinets and to his right, spreading out to an artificial horizon, is a vast open-plan office area.

Young male clerks in white overalls operate metallic gray flexowriter machines. Punched tape coils down into hoppers as stock orders are typed on the machines in quadruplicate. Hans senses that he has been deliberately maneuvered into an *archaic* section where sixties fashions predominate. He believes that he will not inspect the computer and word-processor unit.

No one looks up from his work. Hans might easily be invisible. There are no quilts or stereo systems stored in this area although in the glass cases are packages of what he assumes are cosmetics. Everything in these cabinets is wrapped in plain brown paper but the parcels do vary in size.

Hans is certainly not going to bring himself to murmur: "interesting." A sign on the wall states: Silent work is the best work.

Hans is wearing high leather boots with very thick crepe soles. He can move as silently as any animal. Hans does so. If this is his work he can do it well.

But a man approaches who makes Hans feel badly dressed. In his own plaid jacket and denim trousers Hans would not be out of place in a deer-hunting group in the hills of his south island. The executive who now gestures to Hans wears a dark navy suit of such impeccable cut that it is almost impossible to imagine that the coat and trousers could have emerged from a bolt of material. A close examination of the lapels of the jacket reveals that the suit is hand-stitched from quality worsted.

Hans is waved into the executive's office. He is presented with a cigar and an expensive brandy.

"Are you married back in your own country?"

"Well—no."

"Simply a detail for our publicity department." The executive pressed a button on his desk. "And the brandy . . . ?"

"Excellent."

"So!"

The two men looked at each other.

"Not all of us are dull men," the executive said after a pause, "we dream . . . that is why we command. But we dream in proper sequence—we respect our own time."

Hans smiled and sipped his brandy. His cigar had gone out but he did not like to mention this small inefficiency.

"A man like you," the executive swung in his chair and gazed toward an interior window, "does not require a lecture on the civet cat." They both laughed abruptly.

"You want to see beyond and through musk, ambergris, and myrrh—cut through to the center."

The executive moved from his chair to the window through which a gray light penetrated. He looked out silently and then he called to Hans.

"Come here!"

It was a scene familiar from old British wartime films. A rain-swept street. Women hurrying home with thinly stocked shopping bags. A child pushing a cart which contained two or three lumps of precious coal. Two figures on watch in a doorway wearing leather coats.

"I didn't know it was raining," Hans said.

"It isn't," the executive laughed.

"Your film?" Hans queried.

"Precisely." The executive touched a control. Sunshine burst in the street below.

"One of our testing environments." The German produced a lighter and held it to Hans's cigar.

"What are your plans? You could go a long way with us."

"I'm looking."

"Excellent. I'd ask neither more nor less of you at this juncture."

"At what point will you?" Hans asked.

But the executive was already back at his desk. He began work immediately on a flow chart. Hans walked slowly to the door conscious again of his bulky clothing.

"You would naturally have to become a citizen." The executive's voice was soft. He had not looked up from his diagrams.

"We'll get back to each other, later."

The first naked person he sees is a holographic image. Hans has been in the factory so long that he is not surprised. His body heat, footfalls, gravity, have created specific scenes as he moved in corridors, entered blank warehouse facilities. Hans is also convinced now that his visitor's tag is imprinted with a magnetic code which will allow only particular events to occur.

She is young, golden brown, lying in midair behind a gilt machine gun. A hidden spray emits a cloud of jasmine scent around his head. The girl feeds an endless belt of lipstick cartridges into the breech of the gun. The Schmeisser fires bursts of color at a white screen.

Kreffeld passes his hand through her body. He feels a curious warmth. The girl turns her head towards him and smiles. She is clear to him in every tight curl of hair, each minute blemish of skin. Her lower incisors are slightly crossed and there are beads of sweat down the long channel of her spine.

"Can we talk?" Hans says. Her smile does not immediately change.

"There is a delayed response of a few seconds. It is possible." She pauses. "Permitted."

"Where are you?" Hans waits.

"In the audiovisual center."

"But what are you doing?"

The girl turns her head after a moment. She is watching someone out of the range of his sight. Her eyes have a long focus.

"Advertising." Her voice takes on a note of concern. "You are very close to my space. There are problems in holding the laser beam."

The barrel of the machine gun extends down the corridor. She presses the trigger again. Swollen clouds of color race back toward her down the barrel. Her body explodes silently in a burst of golden light.

Hans feels her disembodied voice close to his ear.

"Go your way."

Moments later Hans removes his visitor's tag. He drops it into an air vent in the corridor floor.

Kreffeld stumbles through clouds of steam in the decontamination center. A figure dressed in white vinyl, head covered completely in a transparent dome, pushes him violently to one side. Hans is driven by a high-pressure jet of hot water. He slips on the tiles which surround the swimming pool and falls, rolling, into the shallow end. He is surrounded by naked figures with blank faces. They grab for his clothing. He knows that these are the models from the *Vogue* magazine although some of them are young males. Their eyse are closed.

He cannot keep his balance in these boots. Hans removes the right one and then, aiming carefully, he hurls it through the steam toward the vinyl-uniformed figure. A stream of hot water catches him in the chest and hurls him backward into the arms of a naked youth. Hans turns quickly. The boy has an erection.

Hans moves, barefooted now, toward the concrete steps at the deep end. He evades another jet of water and scrambles back to the tiled area.

Human mannikins are lodged in each cubicle. They are being smeared with detergent. Guards in their waterproof uniforms are scrubbing at pubic areas and heads.

His breath is bursting his chest. Hans runs toward glassed double doors. A white rubber boot trips him and he falls through the doors on hands and knees.

Kreffeld is photographed in that position. His head turning up toward the light. Hans is photographed again and again. The golden girl uses an old bellows-model Voigtlander. He turns over on his back and gazes at the ceiling from which arc lights glare. The glow erases any suggestion that there might be a trap door there.

"Close your eyes," the girl says.

Distantly, a siren begins to sound in the cosmetic factory.

Hans is dressed in a golden frock. If we turn the pages of the magazine slowly and look carefully we can see the shadow of facial hair under the thick make-up; the eye-shadow is smeared at the corners.

On one photograph, kept in the personnel files in the factory archives, there is a flicker of expression in the eyes.

"Such things," the executive told him, "are best kept to ourselves. Those who rise are those who see and disobey. And that disobedience is a force which most of the workers and models will never understand. But with it we'll change the face of the world. It is life—imagination."

Hans emerges into Germany dressed in a navy suit of impeccable cut. The lapels are hand stitched.

Dressed as he is and with that recorded look in his eyes he will never require a passport. Memories of volcanic hills disappear rapidly.

Our last vision of Kreffeld is of him entering the rear compartment of a company Mercedes. The upholstery is of hand-sewn leather whose color and texture is bafflingly obscure.

There is a momentary problem in lighting his cigar. The executive leans over him and strikes a match. The pupils of Hans's eyes contract, almost disappear.

"Never for one moment did I doubt that your papers would be in order."

But at night Kreffeld dreams of an elegantly restored house. Of a certain way of moving, of climbing.

The chimneys of the cosmetic factory smoke endlessly into the night.

TWO POEMS

ALEKSIS RANNIT

LINE

—Oh yes, I was humble
when young. I too
was born on Samos,
Rhoekos and Mnesikles
my masters.
A day-old colt, I ran
to our spring
on Cape Kantharion
to rinse off the
birth-bloom;
a year-old boy, I was
permitted to pour
a flask of
diaphanous incense
on Hera's altar.
I too dreamt
of conquering
the line-silence of
art in metal and stone,
but, alas,
I steamed with *song*.
(Was I an unburnt phoenix
who would sing
one jubilant line that

bears no illness,
tears, or death?)
Truly,
I thirsted to praise
magnanimous men, but
could not make
a single lyric for
our prince Polykrates.
I needed no
set theme.

At length, lowly,
I longed to give
life to a
pure and hard line
glowing through a
downward mirrored hymn—
like the cool young sun
through a
night-filled seashell;
and yet
another line,
the line of unforced freedom,
line of the Samian sail—
saffron striped with
green—a line like you,
Laníke.
A line to you, Laníke—
linen beaten soft
upon our stream-stones
and dyed with deep-voiced
Tyrian purple.
Or would you hold
in your hand
a round line from Paros
sparkling with new,
living marble?—
The straight line
tall in its splendor,

resembling a spirited
Thessalian horse?
Line   singing warmly
in bleak eternal bronze—
the bare simple line
breathing strict truth
and making warriors
cry?

—Autumn sets in, Laníke,
and the word
rather than wording
loses its prize.
My proud
fourteen-stringed
Korinthian kithara
is no longer with me, only
my silent shepherd's pipe.
I no longer want to hear
harsh lines
of unmelted metal,
square shouldered,
strong thighed   or even
the felicitous lines
showing the flute-girls'
tinted breasts through
innocent, lapis-lazuli-light
Phoinikian tissue.

In Great
remembered Greece, in
Panormos and Tauromenía
the huge
rising sun bursts laughing
along the sea (Why did I not
make for you
a flying line
from the dropped feathers
of my arrow-pierced

Sikanian song?).
Here, in this place,
tight nocturnal morning
surrounds me.
The blue empty season
hangs this year
no longer late, and I
am the lost
summer cicada.
My master now
is the grayish rustle
of the laurel grove
by the river,
my truest friend—
the half-awakened road
in the faint false light.

Do you hear Samian mist
sighing softly with lyres
and sensuous trained voices?—
it is my
ever-postponed
tuneless line
for you, Laníke,
line of whispered promise,
elusive and fragile
line—fallen cadence of
the high sad note,
line—frightened child
clinging to you.

Anakreon's broken-hearted stele
by the roadside
in black winter rain:
I bow gravely,
summoning
silence.

EPILOGUE: In the sixth century B.C. the island of Samos, here the author's imagined birthplace, was home of notable sculptors, architects, poets, and scholars. Some of them, like Rhoekos, the bronze sculptor, and Mnesikles, the architect of the Akropolis's Propylae and probably of the Erechteion, were Samian; others, like the poet Anakreon, worked on the island for decades. (The author lived on Samos in 1959). / Cape Kantharion, with its sacred spring, is situated on the west coast of Samos. / In honor of the goddess Hera, the Samians erected three large temples, calling them Heraions. / Polykrates, the ruler of Samos from *c.* 540 B.C. till 522, was called a "tyrant" in Ancient Greece, a title not suggesting the modern meaning of a despotic exercise of power, but simply denoting any non-hereditary chief of state. Polykrates contributed greatly to the enrichment and civilization of Samos. / Laníke is a love-name for Nike. / "Tyrian purple"—Tyre (or Tyros), the Phoenician island-city, was famous for the production of purple. / Great Greece (*not* Greater Greece)—The south of Italy and the eastern part of Sicily carried this name in antiquity, indicating that especially in the Archaic and Hellenistic periods the true, culturally significant Greece was located there and not on the Greek mainland or the Aegean islands, Syracuse being more civilized than Athens. / Panormos—the ancient name for Palermo; Tauromenía—an ancient name for Taormina; / Sikania—the name of Sicily in archaic times. / Following the recent trend in transliteration, the author uses "k" in place of "c" in Greek names, for example, *K*orinth, not *C*orinth.

TO MARINA TSVETAEVA

Are you   the fruit of
intemperate fire, Marina?
I   cannot paint you. My
color, the rocky soil,
is ashen and slow and
timid in nordic dullness,
my ardor is cold:
refinement of passion—or not?

Are you   the fruit? I would need
the grays   that glimmer
to rose   and melt into faint
green clearing   and
I would need

crimson and lilac and orange
and lusty yellows,
and the lacquer of
many-blossomed blues.

I would need   black
to light you still   deeper
into the wings of
our winter trees. But today
my lines have tired, sharp-
cornered features,
my strongest colors
have overdelicate
quite nervous
hands, and restless eyes.

Can I suppress detail   or sacrifice drawing?
Are you   the fruit
of measured fire, my grief?

NOTE: Marina Tsvetaeva (1892–1941), Russian Expressionist poet, left Russia in 1922 and returned in 1939, lured by the Soviet secret police. In 1941 she hanged herself. Tsvetaeva was greatly admired by Rainer Maria Rilke and Boris Pasternak, among others, and, more recently, Joseph Brodsky proclaimed her the greatest twentieth-century Russian poet.

LA HUMANIDAD

MACLIN BOCOCK

For Yelena and Andrei Sakharov

The palms along the Malecon lean away from the sea. Their fronds move neither up nor down but hang horizontal and always pointing toward the Field of Cinders. The steady, unchanging wind which holds them there never touches us or the Bay. Not a hair on our heads is lifted, not a ripple appears on the water. At least that is what everyone in the Territory believes, everyone except José. Now José is dead. No one listened to him, his voice weak, his body undistinguished. But when I watched the eyes in his dull face burn I knew he saw beyond the Bay, beyond the Field of Cinders. He dared to speak of other possibilities, other ways. He taught me what to listen for, and he showed me things the villagers refused to see. And it was José who begged me to nourish the colt. By law our dead must be interred with ceremony. But I was not allowed to speak. I am not of age and I am female. José's grave remains unmarked.

Yes, it was he who spoke of the colt. It struggles in the flowerless meadow beyond the village border at the edge of the Forbidden Frontier. I go each day to observe its progress. Near the end when I was fanning José's burns, when I was trying to make them less painful, it was then he revealed the place where blades of grass still grow and begged me to care for the colt.

Little changes in the village. The women wait beyond the Hill, always in sight of the shack. Only now José as well as Maria is gone. For a long time the men complained about Maria, wrinkled, whiskers embracing her chin. When she lost her last tooth, when it became embedded in the rotten and half-eaten ear of corn thrown by one of the villagers, they found their justification. She was forced across the road into the Field of Cinders. José tried to stop them. The men shoved him aside. But he was able to slip the stones into her ancient hand. He managed to do this before that giant of a man, his left arm withered, Hernandez, tossed him back a hundred meters toward the Plaza. Yes, they sent Maria away with only one thin and soiled blanket and a rusty pot for boiling water. Now she is invisible, a speck, sometimes moving, but almost imperceptibly, on the Horizon.

It was a rat. I too saw its tail in the rubble of the collapsed bridge. I even glimpsed one furry leg. The few villagers who bothered to come did not notice me, a child. They laughed at José. "Dreamer." They touched their heads. "Idiot." Only a stick, they said, trapped between concrete slabs and left there years before by the last tide.

Later it was the shadow sweeping across the ground bringing the cool freshness. José pulled my head back gently and I saw the bird, a gull, its huge wings spread. I watched as it climbed higher and higher and then descended in widening circles until its shadow had touched the whole Territory. When José called, the villagers dozing on the dilapidated benches around the Zocalo awoke. "Where?" they demanded. "There! There!" José pointed, following with his finger the flight of the bird. Angry, they yelled: "Fraud! Imposter!" and Hernandez, his withered arm curled back on itself, leaned down and slapped José's cheek.

That morning before dawn, when José and I sat huddled together listening and he did not awaken the others, I wondered if he had lost his courage. The donkey brayed until the first rim of the sun showed above the Bay. And one evening, the moon high above us and full, when José failed to arouse the villagers or alert the women or shake the fishermen from their hopeless dreams, I was sure he had become afraid, that he no longer dared. The sound was faint but unmistakable. The dog howled past midnight.

But when the waves came crashing, José, his voice grown even weaker, lost no time in finding me. A child's voice does not carry far. And yet they all came running, even the fishermen who gave up hope long ago, who for years have spent their days and nights on the beach, slumped against decaying boats, their eyes closed. Sun and moonlight blind them. They visit the women only at dusk or before dawn or when the moon has waned. Not that the women are idle. In addition to the service there are the roots to boil, the frayed sacks to mend. But if by chance one of the fishermen is unfortunate, if desire makes demands when the sun is in mid-sky, then he is forced to squint through coarse fingers as he stumbles up the hill and can let his hands fall to his sides only when he is in the windowless shack with the female he has chosen.

Yes, everyone came running. Even the women dared to defy the rules and rushed halfway down the Hill. The waves kept coming and coming, crashing, and all over the Bay fish leaped, silver. Our feet were bathed in foam and the spray flying cooled our faces. Salty drops ran down our cheeks. But they denied it, the villagers, even the fishermen who wanted to believe. The women squatting halfway down the Hill were silent, but the reflection in their eyes was skeptical. When someone spat and snarled, "Betrayer! Criminal!" Hernandez, the only one I fear, for the others have not noticed me, my breasts still small, Hernandez, the humiliating arm twitching, seized José and hurled him upward and out of sight. When José fell back, his crumpled body sank into the stony earth. The villagers turned away and the fishermen, squinting, stumbled to seek their silent boats. And the women fled to their places beyond the Hill.

Hernandez, his arm flapping, dragged me to the Plaza. He forced me up the ruined steps of the roofless and sunken bandstand, its paint peeling, its carved railing gone. I could no longer hear the waves. If I left the circle of rotting timber I would be dispatched. If I continued to believe in José's lies, if I insisted on sharing his illusions, I would be sent beyond the Hill. I would be sent to take Maria's place before my time.

But at siesta when Hernandez began to snore, his arm subdued, I crept back to the beach. There was a thin line of blood across José's forehead. At the edge of the Bay I found the unbroken shell, left, I knew, by the waves. I dipped it into the mute water and when I had washed away the blood, I touched José's right hand and a finger moved. I leaned over his shrunken ear. "I saw the rat's tail," I whispered, "and I watched the gull curve its wings upward. I heard the donkey and I listened to the howling dog and I felt the spray on my face, the salt on my cheeks. I did!" José's lids quivered and between the narrow slits I saw the eyes burning.

Yes, each day at siesta when Hernandez began to snore, I left the deserted bandstand. I moved backward down the treacherous steps, always careful to place my feet where I had first put them. Hernandez still appears in the early morning, his arm restless, and throws me a torn root. He never fails to bend his strong body. He inspects to be sure there are no fresh footprints. He acts on his own. The villagers know nothing of my confinement. They would not be interested. Nor do the fishermen know. They would not care. The women? They learned long ago to mind their own business.

Yes, each afternoon I went to measure José's strength. It was the time the siesta lasted all day, the yearly celebration the reason for which no one remembered, the special day when even the women were allowed to close their eyes, to ignore the tasteless roots, to forget the torn sacks. When the fishermen could dream and redream their tragic histories through long hours, and Hernandez could deny his shameful arm, could thrust it from him under the straw. The hours when the ceaseless snores rolled back and forth across the sleeping villagers, it was then I found José gone. I knelt by the outline of his abused body left in the earth.

But he had not forgotten me. An arrow made of pebbles pointed westward toward the Failed Pyramid, and it was there, where twisted metal was piled on shards of rubber and melted glass, where broken nails and headless screws lay unwanted by tools bereft of sharpness, where the shell of an ancient machine, its wheelless chassis ignored by time, leaned against the circle of orange dust. . . . It was there I came upon José. His hands were raw, bleeding, his mouth toothless, and his body shrunk to half its lean size. But the machine was upright, cleansed of the crusted sand, the steering wheel, faint but visible; the unoiled instruments glowing.

Yes, I found José there. I came upon him pouring in the dark liquid and I saw the floating motes of orange dust. "They will ignite!" I cried. "You must wait," I begged. José shook his head. There was no time left for draining the tank, searching for impurities. But he was mistaken. It was not yet the moment for the bell in the forgotten tower to ring.

I watched José climb the swaying ladder with its rungs missing. I saw him sink into the hole where once a seat had been. I heard the creaky belt pulled from the dangling roller and I listened to the rusty key turn. "The last hope," I thought. I did not know about the colt.

The explosion settled on what was left of the Pyramid. But José would not let me come near him until the cloud of flame had drifted across the road to the Field of Cinders. I could not take a step until the cyclone of smoke had disappeared underground. No, I was not allowed to lift him from the wreckage until the ashes had ceased to murmur.

I laid José in the shadow of the undisturbed circle of dust. It was then, when I was fanning the burns, that he made with his charred finger the feeble signs in the air. It was then that I learned where the few blades of grass still grow and that he begged me to nourish the colt. And it was the moment, too, when the bell in the forgotten tower began to ring, its ancestral sound ending the fiesta of extended sleep.

Yes, Maria has been banished to the horizon and José laid in an unmarked grave and I am detained in this diseased and depraved bandstand. But I do not despair. Before the villagers remark, before some fisherman through squinting eyes notices my enlarging breasts, before the women whisper, "Soon she will be here, among us," I will have fled this round of sinking wood and I will have left the flowerless meadow. For the colt gathers strength, too. It has turned on its side, its legs no longer point stiffly upward. The mane is beginning to grow thick and glossy and each afternoon when I put a blade of grass in its mouth, the tongue becomes warmer.

No, it will not be long before we escape, before we cross, the colt and I, the Forbidden Frontier.

TWO POEMS

PABLO ANTONIO CUADRA

Translated from the Spanish by Steven White

THE CALABASH TREE

> *In memory of Pedro Joaquín Chamorro,*
> *whose blood made Nicaragua conceive her freedom*

    A hero rebelled against the powers of the Black House.
A hero struggled against the masters of the House of Bats,
against the masters of the House of Darkness
                                  —*Quequma-ha*—
where, inside, there are only sinister thoughts.
The Mayas called him *Ahpú* which means "chief" or "head"
because he led the way. And it was his bold foot that broke
        new ground.
Often he succeeded in ridiculing the oppressors,
but finally he fell in their hands.

    (Shadows! I have lost a friend!
Village rivers cry beside his remains.
The old fortune-tellers prophesied a time of desolation.
"It will be," they said, "a sad, sad time
in which butterflies will be gathered"
and words will no longer transmit the golden pollen.
I imagined it as a time of treacherous light—

a cold, dying sun and the long caws of birds
pecking at autumn.
But it was a morning, a false shining
of blue joy, the fresh
songs of the birds and then
                              the trap!
the dry blow of the deadfall
that suddenly crushes
the smiling, unaware hero.)

"You will be destroyed, broken to pieces,
and here your hidden memory will remain,"
said the masters of the House of Obsidian
(whose barracks was the House of Weapons).
And they decapitated the liberator.
And they ordered that his head be placed on a sharpened pole,
and suddenly the pole became a tree
covered with leaves and fruit
and the fruit resembled human heads.
    On this tree, I write:
Crescentia cújete
Crescentia trifolia
Xicalli in the Nahuatl tongue
the calabash tree
with leaves like crosses:
fasciculated, beautiful
leaves with a sacrificial design,
a memorial to martyrs,
"the tree of skulls."

This is the plant
that gives dignity to the plains.
Its fruit is the Indians' cup.
The *campesinos* call its fruit *el quacal* or *la jícara*
                    —*the cup of all we drink*
and carve birds on it for decoration
                    —*because we drink the song*
The fruit rattles in our fiestas as maracas and *sonajas*
                    —*because we drink the music*
Since ancient times, in the dialect of the Chorti Maya,

the word *Ruch* meant both
"calabash" and "head" (just as it does for us)
                    —*because we drink thoughts*

   But the masters of Darkness
                    (the censors)
said, "Let no one approach this tree.
Let no one dare pick this fruit."

And a girl whose name was Blood Girl knew this history.
   The
maiden bravely asked,
"Why can't I know this tree's miracle?"
And she jumped over the oppressors' words of warning
and approached the tree.
She approached the tree so that the myth
could bring us together in its image:
because the woman is the freedom that provokes action
and the hero is the unhindered will.

"Ah!" she exclaimed. "Will I live or die if I pick
   this fruit?"
Then the fruit spoke, one of the heads among
   the branches spoke.
"What do you want?
Don't you know that these are the heads of the sacrificed?
Could it be that you want them?"
And the maiden replied, "Yes. I want them!"
"Then you must reach out your right hand!" said the head.
And the maiden reached out her hand.
And the skull spit on her palm.
The saliva disappeared at once and the tree spoke.
"In my saliva, I have given you my ancestry.
Because the word is blood
and blood is once again the word."

And this is how our first civilization began
—A tree bore witness—
This is how the dawn begins and germinates each time
like Blood Girl, the maiden who begat

Hunter and Jaguar Deer
from the hero's courage.
They were the twins who invented Corn—
the bread of America, the grain
that becomes the communion of the oppressed.

THE COCOA TREE

To Juan Aburto
    They used to drink it with flowers.

In a polished gourd bowl, whipped until it was frothy.
It was like drinking the earth:
    a bittersweet
    drink.
Linnaeus calls it *Theobroma:* food of the gods.
Oviedo, the Chronicler of Nicaragua, finds it "precious
    and healthy"
"And the Indians say that if you drink cocoa while fasting
    no snake or serpent will bite you."
But Benzoni, the Italian, rejects it: "It seems like a brew
    better fit for dogs than people."
En route, Columbus discovered a big canoe with Indians
    transporting cocoa.
The distant tribal chiefs of the Caribbean bartered gold and jade
    for the seeds of the cocoa tree.
Anne of Austria carried the fragrant drink in her wedding
    at the French Court.
And Doctor Juan de Cárdenas, the viceroys' physician,
    found the drink contradictory:
"Cold, dry, earthy and
melancholy and also light, bland, soothing and loving."
This is why Madame de Sévigné, moving like a gull in her salon,
    drinks from a fine porcelain cup and pronounces:
        "This drink acts according to the wishes of the person who
            drinks it."
And Reverend Bruce in London takes a puritan sip of chocolate
    and says, "It is an aphrodisiac more dangerous than a novel."

In the *Güegüence* toasts are made with *tiste* not with wine.

Now we are raw material. The price of cocoa is on
    Wall Street's blackboards.

And Ezra, in his canto: "With usury . . . the peasant does not
    eat his own grain."
The tribal chief, don Francisco Nacatime, told his son,
    "If you want to be rich, plant some cocoa trees."
But he died poor. The tree
    plays with its great, oval-shaped, alternate leaves.
    Then it is covered with a lateral flowering—
    thousands of small reddish or yellow blossoms like stars.
And the flowers fall and only a few give birth to "the great
    mazorcas
    of the cocoa tree, green and lit with red"
    with five cells of seeds
    wrapped in a juicy pulp.
But it is a demanding tree. And delicate.
    "It only lives in a warm, shadowy place
    and it dies if the sun touches it."
This is why they always plant a mother cocoa tree beside it
    to cover it with a giant shadow like an angel.
Because it is one of the trees of Paradise
    and requires, like freedom, an arduous and permanent
        cultivation.
Its name comes from *caua* (to take a long time) and *ca-caua*
    (to take a very long time)
    because it isn't a wild plant, but a gift from Quetzalcoatl
    to the people who chose freedom.
    Before the Toltecs and the Mayas
when Quetzalcoatl wasn't a god but a man among us,
when flowers and butterflies instead of people were sacrificed
    to the gods,
Quetzalcoatl told us, "We are a wandering people."
And he gave us a drink called *pinol*, made from corn.
And he gave us *tiste*, a drink made from cocoa and corn.
Drinks for the pilgrims.
Because ours is the land of the uprooted.

We are the people whose only Country is called freedom.
> But the Nahuas came.
> I cross roads where tractors
unearth burial mounds. This is where their bones remained.
*(Grandfather: you are burdened with the memory of your people
and it is as heavy as a load of stones)*
This is where their footprints remained. Toltecs. Craftsmen.
Fragments of a polychromatic amphora as exquisite as a
 Greek urn.
(Grandfather: What fire do your flints light?) And I read
in the Book of Origins, in the annals of the sons of Tula:
Year 1 Acatl. Year of sorrow.
The Olmecs fell upon our lands.
Strong leather helmets covered their heads.
Armor of thick cotton covered their chests.
An arch of falling arrows covered them like an awning as they
 advanced.
Groups of men with clubs followed the archers.
And in the rear guard, chubby dwarfs with obsidian knives
sprouted from the earth to finish off the defeated.
And there were no longer pages in our books on which to write
 our history,
only an endless list of our tributes:
One hundred hens per tribe plus one hundred loads of cocoa
One hundred loads of cotton plus one hundred loads of feathers
One hundred loads of corn plus twenty jade stones
And one hundred pieces of pottery and twenty pieces of gold.
And the sons of Tula ate lizards and worms.
And they awaited the night and said to each other,
"Have we castrated the sun that no longer shines?"
And they went to the temple and fasted
and bled their members
and with tears and blood they interrogated their gods
and the gods ordered them to leave.

> This is how those who spoke the Nahuatl tongue undertook
> their exodus.
"You will find a freshwater Sea to the south.
There you will be able to see an island with two volcanoes."

The exiled people went south.
They went south in search of the promised land.
And wherever they came, the people rejected them.
"Who are these people?" they would ask each other.
"Could it be that we know their faces? Don't they carry
 foreign hearts in their chests?"
And the Mayas attacked them with their knives from Zaquitoc.
And the Cakchiquels attacked them with their clubs from
 Guayacán.
And the Sutiavas gave them battle with their lances from
 Huiscoyol.
And the wars produced warrior chiefs.
And the warrior chiefs named a Great Chief.
And the Great Chief did not walk on the earth. He was carried
 in blankets.
And the tyranny of the Olmecs seemed pale
compared to the tyranny of Ticomega, the elder
succeeded by Ticomega, the younger
succeeded by Ticomega, the grandson.

Now we are in the land of lakes.
We were also pilgrims. We were
emigrants and these tired tribes came to our land.
We, the Chorotegas, felt sorry for them when they cried,
"Our people are wounded and sick!" They are Mexicans.
They are Toltecs. They are artists who shape clay and stone.
They are masters in the art of plumage.
They play the ocarina. They work with silver and gold.
They know the stars.
And so we help them carry their things.
We give them our warriors to carry their load.
"We will not stay," they tell us. But the night comes
and the Nahuas imitate the owl with their bird-language.
And they whistle: *Tetec-Tetec* (slash, slash)
And the others answer: *Iyollo-Iyollo* (hearts, hearts)
And this was the signal and they fell upon the carriers.
And after finishing them off with knives, they fell upon us.
And they took the best of our lands from us—
all the cocoa trees in the south!

And as soon as they were the owners of these trees
they used the seeds as money.
The people no longer drank cocoa—
only the *teytes*, the land owners,
only the rich lords and the warrior chiefs.
"And the common people do not dare and cannot use that brew
for their gain or their palates
since it would be nothing more than growing poor on purpose
and swallowing their money."
And one can buy a rabbit for 10 seeds from the cocoa tree
And for 2 seeds one can acquire a dove
A slave is worth 100 seeds
And a woman sells her body for 10.
"What I mean is that *anything* can be sold."

Cocoa:
the dollar
       that grows on a tree.

THE SNOW TUNNEL

MICHAEL McGUIRE

The husband did not recognize the lover at first. And when he did, seeing at the same time his own head in the store's angled shoplifter mirror, he began, irrelevantly he knew, to compare him with himself physically. Two men lined up in the mind of one—one, at least, who was no longer taken with appearances, and held the sex act in a healthy perspective. Nevertheless, he questioned the mirror. Who was grayer now? Who had gone softest around the middle? Which of them looked most satisfactorily out of his eyes, exuding solidness and self? He was always surprised by his own eyes when he came upon them like this, staring unexpectedly out of some wall, already somewhat bemused by this sudden spectacle of humanity, his good self he knew—from within; but from without—a not very tall man who appeared for the moment somewhere somehow out of tune. Or had he only forgotten the melody?

And the lover? How was he now—in there where the soul made what music it had? What crossed his mind when their eyes crossed? (Like rusting swords?) He had recognized the husband first certainly (were those old horns still on his head? he wondered), their eyes sticking together in one of those omnipresent mirrors under the fluorescent lights (did the idea of theft bring anything up?), and the lover's eyes had sent forth no challenge, no claim. They had not even twinkled. Sensitive, intelligent eyes. Not the kind you wanted to knock out of his head—no matter what (or who) they had seen.

And, after a moment, the lover had turned to the small dark woman at his side, for he was with another woman now and had something to share with her. And the husband moved on, following his second wife's inclinations in another direction (he was not at the moment consciously grateful), and no word passed, not even a look that said anything to anybody. After all, the confrontation was twenty years too late. There was no covetousness in the one, no vengeance in the other. They were lost in their own thoughts now, each intent on his own downward path. And no one was trying—with fresh tears and midnight affirmations—to choose between them.

Shall I tell him, he wondered? And then, shall I tell her? He allowed himself to be drawn further down an aisle full of bottles, finishes, and mixes, at one end of which his present wife was examining a new aluminum easel, while at the other the small dark woman was choosing a canvas. The husband, once more caught between two impulses allegedly higher than his own, came to a stop reflecting momentarily on the natural emptiness of woman, her vain attempts to fill the afternoons he purchased for her with art, good works, and another man, with some sensation or affectation of fullness which was always a sham until she was actually plugged-up, bursting at the seams, and the little bastard—who would fill the mornings too, by God—was already sucking on the end of a long tube which ran directly into his pocket.

But his wrath transformed him only for a second—he felt the fire in his nostrils cool and go out—and he found himself sweating absurdly and feeling a little like the old kid on the block, the one who was there first and had had his chance to breathe defiance to the newcomer about ten paces (or twenty years) ago and had missed it. And now . . . ? Now the woman in question had largely forgotten them both, and he saw her forgetful face and he began to wonder, a few years late he knew, just what had gone so irremediably wrong in that long-ago youth they had shared, and he tried to remember.

"What's wrong with you? You look sick." His present wife, gently enough.

"That's one of my wife's lovers over there," he said, almost involuntarily.

"One of your first wife's lovers you mean. I never saw the fellow before."

"Yes. No, I know," he said, partly smiling.

"And you're hiding here behind the little green bottles?" He had heard that note of amusement somewhere. How he had entertained in his time! "Isn't that best forgotten?" she asked quietly.

"I'm wondering if I shouldn't inform him," he said.

"Of what?"

"Of her condition."

Their eyes met, the eyes of the present husband and wife, and the husband reflected that life would go on adding to and subtracting from this man and woman until it was done with them. Too.

"There was a time," he began, wondering if this was an argument and, if so, for what, "a time when our child, hers and mine, used to call me by his name." He felt the broken smile creep halfway across his face.

"And now she wouldn't know who this old fellow was if you told her," she said. And after a moment, "It's up to you," she added, and wandered on filling her basket, and leaving him as somehow young and uncertain on his feet as the groom in a photograph of two people who were no longer married. And again he saw the forgetful face and the young eyes that believed happiness so impossible that they had convinced him. And they were right, of course. Of course . . .

Once upon a time when you were a child, the snow tunnel caved in. You fought wildly, uselessly. Then you lay still. You didn't think you'd ever get out. Now, waking up one drawn-out afternoon, you cannot move. You think you're in the snow tunnel still. The room is white . . .

You were twenty-two once, mother of my child. (We held together long enough for that.)

Then there was the time on the steep bank of a mighty river. I stood on the heights throwing great gobs of snow on you, huge sticky armfuls that shattered on your back, coating your sweater inches thick. But you kept coming with a will, steady, imperturbable, holding onto roots, drawing yourself up like the primeval river woman, until I collapsed in hysterics and you were sitting next to me cleaning the snow from your glasses.

Then we bought a puppy. Whose is it? a friend asked. It's ours, we said. You chose the sex. We fought over the name. Later I got rid of the yelps and the frightened eyes. Gave them away with a case of yellow dog food. After the child three females were too much for me.

And we stood alone on the shores of Lake Superior. It was a bright October day. Brilliant leaves flew all around us. On top of a rock I held you and kissed you and took your blouse off. Later, in the car, you began to sneeze.

And there was the class we met in. You can't forget that. The teacher killed himself years later. (Was it because we once survived his course—and even left it hand in hand?)

Yes, the lake shore and the river bank, an English professor with death in his eyes, the chasings around and the wrestling matches, the cries, the pleasure and the pain. That's it, isn't it? Seconds remembered of a time that took hours, days, years . . . And then? Do you . . . ? Do you remember? Where did impossibility . . .

Once upon a time when you were a child, the snow tunnel caved in. You didn't think you'd ever get out. Now . . .

When I visit our child, it's her fights I have to hear about, it's her child we pass around, her questions that I . . .

"No. I can't tell you about your mother—any more than she could tell you about me. Don't ask. We never knew each other. Or, if we did, we've forgotten."

"Dad . . . !"

"Really. Nothing. I remember nothing."

"Are you all right? You were so still."

"Was I?" The husband looked around him at the fluorescent lights, the shoplifter mirrors, and the full basket in his wife's hands. And he remembered the eyes that believed happiness so impossible, and he wondered if she, his first wife, had known somewhere inside her as a child, as a young woman, that this time was coming and that it would find the husband of her youth, and the lover who had taken his place, unnecessary, irrelevant.

"Are you going to tell him?" his wife asked.

He looked at her again, and the reality of the present came back to stay. People realigned themselves. The past vanished. This was his wife now. His first wife had remarried years ago. Neither he, nor the lover who was buying brushes for the little dark woman, had anything to say to each other. And they were no help at all to the strange figure lying motionless in that white room.

"No, I don't think so," he said.

"Then let's get out of here. I'm suffocating."

The sound of the cash register. The wind ruffling his hair and the first drops of new rain on his face. A hand in his. He stuck the easel under his arm as fathers do with small children sometimes. And silently he sent what hope he had backward—for the sake of a time that wasn't yet forgotten, for a present that must be very difficult, and for a woman he had once loved.

TEN POEMS

PHILIPPE DENIS

Translated from the French by Mark Irwin

1
The day does not let me write—

On this page
I fall to ash
until night.

(Alternating
light and dark of the blinds
—the house is this dream

where I burn
—when the secret of tears
grips me
—salt awakened.

2
Earth—as if I were entering
where a body can no longer live

(day's vow . . . up to the wind

The lure of a drunken star,
will have been the sole enigma
between sky and self . . .

Empty place, where I gain back this body.

3
Alert living
—under sleep's curve.

The lamp's concern where
I stay up—

Your heart, away,
is a date—

. . . unexpected beginning
of an earth
wrinkled at my waking.

4
Star: umbel of this sky,
the color itself
whiteness of all white.

Up to the image
I hold my breath,

dream
bars the wind.

A heart swims
in the blood—free
from all nights.

5
Between self and self—
the road.

The washing lengthens
like shadows.

(Polar bed
of my sleep

6
Through the wound
which reconciles us to the unknown—

I live
without sleep—like a lamp
having the age
of this slope—

Snow uses me
in the night—
to regain its color
on the border
of language.

7
Moored to your blood,
the hollow
left by your sleep,
now breathes
for you—

(wind between the last stars
flows

rooster scruffs
sputters
in the coop—

before roads begin
to swell
—like the veins
of your wrists.

8
I come out of the earth,
everywhere,
like these seeds,

(insect
in the dry obscurity
of wood:

I eat the space
which lies in advance,

I rise back
through the sap's salty course,

drunk,
and blind—

until the season
sets
my leaf blood.

9
    Shadow . . . this axiom of the body—this place where again
I begin (pure angle

                          for shaping my death)
this last will
of gesture—inlaid with dust—
                      tiny heart
                      heart of this inverse life

10
Graven—on the wings of the butterfly,
the equilibrium of dust
sets to bloom—

The alphabet
and flowers,
                announce
new sorrows for you—

(While the seed of the poppy
hems its scarlet wound)

EXPERIENCE

JORGE EDWARDS

Translated from the Spanish by Edith Grossman

It must have been twenty years ago—I was still a teenager—when an Argentinian, an amateur graphologist who was spending the summer in Chile, analyzed my handwriting. "None of your plans will succeed," the Argentinian announced. "You will think you have found your place in life, you will think, after many false starts, that you have finally gotten on the right track, and then suddenly an unforeseen turn of events will destroy everything. You will begin again, you will tell yourself that the new life is really the definitive one, that now you are really moving in the right direction and will never change, and then you will discover that overnight your plans have all gone to hell and you have to start over again from scratch. And so on and so forth. According to your handwriting the only thing left . . ." At this point he hesitated and never finished the sentence.

The Argentinian took graphology seriously; he said these things solemnly, looking into my eyes with great intensity. His seriousness made me laugh, but he didn't change his manner, as if . . . I remember that he refused to take off an enormous scapulary even when he rode the waves. Later, we learned ("we" being the group on the beach who tripped over ourselves in the rush to show him our handwriting) that he was a student of the occult sciences; we also learned that he eventually held an important post in the Perón regime. Some people said that he stole with so much enthusiasm that he could not return to his country. I understand that he is living somewhere in the United States, undoubtedly devoted to magic, esoteric religions, and the enjoyment of his income. But I haven't heard anything else about him for years.

I recalled the predictions of the Argentinian in connection with recent events. Despite arguments, constant recriminations, and an exasperation that was renewed every day under the most varied pretexts, it had never occurred to me that my marriage to Judith could end. But it did end, it was irreparably destroyed, like so many other situations in my life: my engagement to Eliana Sánchez, my friendship with Tulio, my job teaching music history (at the time I thought I had found overwhelming reasons for leaving it, but with the passage of time the reasons have disappeared, all that is visible today is instability, a devouring dissatisfaction, my desire to write a work for the theater . . .) The Argentinian wasn't so wrong after all.

After so many changes I have ended up living alone in a boardinghouse. I have a large, dilapidated room; the wallpaper is covered with water stains. There is an armchair with the springs showing through (the landlady promised to fix it when I took the room—I don't think she ever will), two chairs, one with the wicker broken, a big, ugly, fairly comfortable table where I accumulate papers, books, newspapers, dirty coffee cups, and cigarette butts. The lamp on the night table has to lean against the wall or else it falls over. But the bed isn't bad, the room is spacious, and the two windows look out on a little neighborhood square that I like.

When I left Judith's apartment my mother told me that I could come back to live with her like before I was married. I refused. I've come to the conclusion that I like living alone; it is the only life I do like. I recognize the fact that I have the soul of a bachelor. I read my books, I revise old papers, I prepare my cups of coffee on the gas burner, and I spend hours contemplating the little square. I keep expenses down, and that makes for independence. Judith owns some land planted in oranges and lemons, and she hasn't tried to ask me for money. With my job as a secretary at the company and a few private lessons I have enough, more than enough. My students' laziness used to drive me wild, their stupidity was maddening (they are boys who have fallen behind in their regular classes, and my job is to keep them from failing—at any cost, and by any means) but recently I have acquired patience and a certain methodology: when they don't understand my explanations I don't press them; I make them repeat like automatons the facts most frequently asked for on the examinations; they retain something, and I don't get angry. With this method and a few quiet words to the examiners—especially if the students have influential parents—I've had rather good results.

But I won't go back to my mother's house under any circumstances. At first everything would be fine: all tolerance, mutual respect, special dishes, tickets to the movies, all kinds of tact. But later, as we got used to each other again, the meddling, the arguments would begin: why don't I take a job in a lycée, and why don't I work for some American company with my command of English, and so much coffee is no good for me, and my friends are a bunch of bums, good-for-nothing weaklings . . . Forget it! Nobody moves me from here. I have the soul of a bachelor, and that's just fine with me. In fact, I like this life. The square. My books. The papers I pull out from the bottom of suitcases. The old photographs. Stopping in at the downtown bars without having my mother turn out her light in silent accusation as soon as I come home. Talking with Excipión, with Peralta, with the Worldly Tiger (where'd he ever get that nickname?) over a bottle of wine. And in time there's bound to be a girl who comes to visit me at the boardinghouse: some young teacher fresh from the provinces . . . What more could anyone ask! The predictions of the Argentinian were true for a certain period of my life that is definitely over and done with. The crisis, the rupture, of the last two years were necessary. But that's all past history now. If you think about it carefully there is no reason why instability, a lack of balance . . . maturity invariably . . .

The little square only has six benches, four dusty trees, and a few bushes. The bad thing about the boardinghouse is the smell of cooking, but one gets used to it. The landlady is a fat woman with a mustache and a rather unfriendly look. Her husband, an old invalid Spaniard, hardly ever leaves his room. Behind my room there is a small patio with a chicken coop: eight or ten hens and a rooster with half his feathers gone, an evil disposition, and hard, bloodshot eyes. At about 6:00 in the evening I like to watch them settle down on their roosts to sleep. Edelmira, the youngest maid—she looks like an absolute idiot—appears at the kitchen door and empties a tub of bleach water into the patio. The landlady comes out and walks toward the bedrooms, rattling a keyring. She doesn't deign to notice my presence. Years ago this would have bothered me; now I couldn't care less. I've overcome the sensitivity that used to make me suffer needlessly.

My mother asked me again to come live with her. She gave me all kinds of reasons. At first, the discussion was very calm and sensible; slowly it grew bitter until there was a terrible scene—accusations of ingratitude interrupted by hysterical crying. I told her it wasn't maternal love but pure egotism, and if it continued I'd never set foot in her house again. That really did it. I never imagined she would react like that. She threw a cushion at my head; luckily I jumped just in time to grab the opaline lamp she hit instead. Then she tried to throw me out, pushing and shoving me. I had to hold her hands, force her to sit down, call the maid to give her a tranquilizer. She drank the medication, sobbing disconsolately, and she told me that she was feeling very lonely, that for a woman of her age the worst thing was solitude, that a grandchild would have brought joy to her life but now . . . Had to stay with her until midnight. My impatience to get out of that house had never been so great. There was some port left, and I drank it all.

"Next time have something drier for me," I told her. "Wine, even if it's . . ."

She agreed; her face was a *mater dolorosa*'s. But I wasn't in the mood to be impressed; I felt lucid despite her tactics, and that gave me a kind of immunity. We spoke about the deputies' election, about taxes, about my boardinghouse.

"After two weeks I've found two things wrong with it: the smell of cooking and the rooster."

"The rooster?"

"Yes; it wakes me every morning at five."

"All right," she said, looking at the floor with a bitter expression, "I won't insist. You know exactly what you're doing."

Foreseeing a new outburst, I stood up. I said that I had to be at work early the next day. I kissed her on the forehead and on the cheeks and patted her affectionately.

"Are you coming tomorrow?"

"I don't know. Maybe the day after."

I watched her stoically swallow her bitterness.

"If I can get away early," I lied to her, "I'll come for a little while."

"Come for supper," she said.

"I don't know. I'd rather not commit myself."

On the street I realized I wasn't feeling well; the port and the rough time I'd had with her had upset my stomach. I met Peralta in the Iris Café, and I talked to him about my mother; her loneliness made me sad, but there wasn't much I could do to help her. Peralta surprised me with a moralizing sermon on filial duty. It was a side of him that I'd never seen before. But in any event the sermon didn't keep us from drinking two bottles of red wine. At about 1:30 we were joined by a friend of Peralta's, a rather unpleasant cross-eyed man. We ordered bread, some pepper sauce, and another bottle. His friend ate and drank like a pig and of course never offered to pay. Peralta told funny stories about his service in the Merchant Marine. I got to the boardinghouse at 3:40; the acid was eating holes in my stomach, and I calculated that I'd only get five hours of sleep. I had a student at 9:30—one of the hardest ones, an absolute idiot, a blockhead. I set the alarm, undressed quickly, and fell into bed like a stone.

I was walking with a tall gray-haired woman through a garden where there were many people: children jumping all around us without looking at us, serious-looking men sitting on the grass holding gloves and top hats. We knew that there was a leopard at the bottom of the garden, but nobody mentioned it, as if any allusion to it would be in bad taste. The woman's conversation had a soothing effect; it produced an ineffably deep feeling in me.

At first the rooster's crowing was one of the sounds in the garden. Then it detached itself from those noises, it grew and grew, and finally it established itself, alone and sharp, in all the barrenness of dawn, in the exact center of my startled nerves, and the taste of metal in my mouth, and my aching head. He kept crowing; when he finally stopped there was no hope of falling asleep again. The wheels of the trolley car pulverized my brain. The creaking of the floorboards was like being buried alive in splinters. The precise, incisive ring of the first footsteps on the street. An occasional car. The noise of the plumbing . . . He crowed again, and I could have strangled him. I decided to talk to the landlady. It was impossible! What kind of boardinghouse was it? Señora, you have no right! After all, I pay you money so that I can sleep in peace . . .

Since I felt so bad yesterday I decided to wait until today to talk to the landlady. When I don't feel well I prefer to avoid difficult situations. Last night I slept from exactly 10:00 p.m. to 5:00 a.m. That's when the rooster woke me again. All right, I should have expected it. I read for a while, but my nerves wouldn't let me concentrate; at the end of the first chapter I couldn't tell one character from another, I didn't know who they were or where they came from. Then I got up and went down to the courtyard to look at the rooster; I wanted to see him crow, see him throw back his neck and hurl himself wholeheartedly into a resounding, vibrating convulsion. He showed no signs of doing anything; it seemed to me that with his stubborn refusal he clearly intended to deny me pleasure. I went out for a walk around the little square (I still liked it). Except for the early sparrows and a bum stretched out on a bench there was no one there. A guard came up, intending to question the bum, and then he decided it was better not to complicate his life.

I came back from my walk at about 7:00. The landlady, who was feeding the chickens, greeted me with bad humor. I suspected that my irregular hours irritated her: going to bed one day at 5:00 a.m. and getting up the next day at 6:00.

"Your rooster doesn't let me sleep," I said to her.

She continued throwing corn, not answering me.

"I don't know about the others, but as far as I'm concerned . . ."

Her huge shoulders bending over the chicken coop were her only answer. I was rooted to the spot, hopelessly looking for the threat that would have some effect, and I ended up shrugging my shoulders. What was the point of talking to her?

"Is breakfast ready?"

"At 7:30," she answered, "like always."

I went into my room and fixed some strong coffee on the gas burner. I tried reading again but it was impossible. The boardinghouse was becoming openly hostile. After two and a half weeks of living there three really major problems had clearly emerged: the rooster, the landlady, and the smell of cooking. But the spacious room and the little square with its four trees and its scruffy bushes still offered some consolation.

Yesterday when I was downtown I ran into Wilcox, a friend from college, and he told me that Judith was seeing someone else. I recognize the fact that the news upset me. More than I would ever have imagined. I think I turned pale, and I felt my legs go weak.

"It's only natural," I said, making an effort so that my voice would not betray me, "what did you expect?"

Wilcox didn't take his bird-eyes off me—grayish-blue eyes surrounded by innumerable premature wrinkles; he was trying to penetrate my apparent indifference . . . He is unmarried, on his way to becoming a confirmed bachelor; his rich little girlfriend jilted him. Yesterday, behind his false gringo innocence, he behaved with a refined malice. I have no doubts about that. I managed to control myself, and I suspect that Wilcox was frustrated because of it. He began to rant and rave about the bureaucrats, the Masons, the people in Parliament. They were insatiable: the only thing they knew how to do was raise their own salaries and travel around the world at the taxpayers' expense! I asked him to excuse me but I was in a hurry, and I left him in the middle of a sentence. The truth is that the news hit me like a blow to the head. I was stunned, I was almost run over crossing the street (I accepted the insults of a cab driver and a cyclist), somehow I made my way to my mother's house. She complained bitterly about the electric bills, the food bills; she tried to prove to me that if we lived together our total expenditures would be significantly reduced: I would finally be able to buy some clothes, she would be able to get a rug for her bedroom. She had heard of a Jew where the rugs . . .

"You know what?" I said to her. "I heard Judith's been going out with another man. A lawyer, it seems."

It was hard for her to change the subject. Once she realized what I had said to her she shrugged her shoulders and clasped her hands.

"Yes, well," I remarked, interpreting her thought. "What can you do?"

She shook her head:

"What can you do? It's just as well you didn't have children . . ."

"Just as well!"

For a while we were silent.

"Well," she continued. "What did you expect? Maybe it's for the best. Maybe it will keep you from having any more illusions."

"I don't have any illusions," I protested indignantly. "Where'd you get the idea that I have any illusions?"

My mother went to check on dinner, and I began to pace up and down between the living room and her bedroom; I remembered moments from my life with Judith, her expressions, fragments of sentences, the sound of her voice, her laughter. I saw her walking across the carpet, arranging the flowers that helped to justify our living room, yawning, immune to my repeated, stubborn, confused demands . . . "Don't be a bore . . . Can't you see I'm dead tired?" I tried to imagine her in the relaxed moments of our love-making, but the images slipped away. My mother came back from the kitchen, and we sat down at the table. To change the subject I talked about the rooster at the boardinghouse waking me at 5:00 every morning. She spoke of the dog who belonged to the ladies on the second floor; he jumped at her on the stairs and scared her to death . . .

"But that rooster is maddening! One of these nights I'll wring his neck!"

I re-created the landlady's face, and the hateful crowing of the rooster, the livid dawns, the grinding wheels of the streetcars, the first footsteps on the sidewalk. I banged the table, unable to control a fit of anger. My mother raised her eyes in alarm.

"The next time I'll wring his neck!"

"I've told you a thousand times," she interrupted. "You have the solution at hand. But . . ."

I decided it was the better part of valor to talk about my classes. The ideal place for them, when all was said and done, was the boardinghouse: there was room, and it was quiet—the rooster rarely crowed during the day. Looking up from the textbook and contemplating the little square was very restful . . .

I left early and walked downtown. I didn't find anyone at the usual places. I killed a lot of time; when I had just about given up hope I met Peralta's cross-eyed friend in the doorway of the Iris Café. I really wanted company, so I invited him to share a bottle of wine with me. We talked about all kinds of things. The cross-eyed friend declared that Fidel Castro had betrayed the revolution, that he had become a slave of the Soviet Union. I wasn't in the mood to discuss anything. Then he said that the Americans were a bunch of infants and that the only people worth anything in Europe were the Germans: just look how they had rebuilt their industries! Convinced that the most sensible thing would be to go to bed, I was debating whether to invite him to have another bottle when Peralta walked in. We called a waiter immediately, and the second bottle was quickly dispatched. By the third bottle I told them what I had found out about my ex-wife.

"What did you expect?" exclaimed Peralta, "that she would be faithful to you after you had separated? Women have the same needs that we do. It's a law of nature."

In order to tolerate this absolutely direct version of the situation I had to drink down my glass of wine in one swallow. I felt tired, and a desire for sleep penetrated my deepest being; I wanted to lie down and sleep for hours on end. I felt the vibrant red crest, the hard eyes, heard the vicious cry that I would gladly have strangled with my last ounce of strength. After the fifth bottle, paid for by Peralta, I stood up with determination despite the protests of the cross-eyed man. I took a taxi to the boardinghouse. I opened the door quietly, and instead of going to my bedroom I went into the courtyard.

The light of the waning moon, darkened by gray clouds, weakly illuminated the rooster, who was sleeping among his concubines. Fascinated, I looked at him from behind the wire. The night breeze, together with the delayed effects of the wine, produced a semiecstatic state in me. I opened the little door and went in; my steps were not very firm, but all my doubts, my vacilations, my uncertainties had disappeared. I touched my enemy's feathers with my fingertips, almost caressing him. Then, very gently, I moved my hands toward his neck, made sure they went around it, and with an intense effort to gather the energies that had been dissipated by wine, I squeezed furiously, certain that the whole procedure would take only a few seconds. The rooster stretched and flapped its wings, sluggishly at first (I thought for a moment that this would be his final death agony), and then with a sudden, frenetic vigor that took me completely by surprise. I was about to let him go—the wine made me react slowly—but I caught myself in time and increased the pressure, trying to wring his neck. The bird kept flapping his wings; he seemed to float and me along with him; I had a fleeting vision of his eyes hardened by a hateful will to survive. I even thought I heard his cry of alarm.

From that moment on my memory of the scene is very confused. I know that the thought of his crowing—waking the whole boardinghouse, making me look like an absolute fool—strengthened my purpose. Several times I made a supreme effort, calling on all my reserves of strength, and still I couldn't overpower him. I don't know if it took me five minutes or three quarters of an hour to finish him off. What I do remember clearly is throwing away a lifeless bundle that stuck to my hands while the perspiration soaked through my shirt. I kicked the bundle into a corner of the chicken coop. I think I covered it with earth. Trembling, with my heart beating wildly, I went into my room. Little by little the soporific effect of the wine took hold again. I calmed down. Finally, at 3:00, I sank into bed with a deep voluptuousness, ready to make up for so many miserable dawns.

Tunnels, staircases, bats, damp slippery objects, I lost my footing, the stairs were rotting, water and moss on walls that had never seen the light, and I was beginning to fall into the well that was opening up, I had to move my arms, to fly, but the leaden fatigue, the abyss was getting closer, it was surrounding me, its black covering, dizzy, impossible to grab hold of anything solid, the rotting boards fell too, the surface of the wall, slimy, my wings were heavy, they knocked against the walls . . . At a quiet moment in the dream the crowing of a cock was heard over and over again. It made its way through the shadows. And suddenly the raw light again through the window while the clock on the night table read 5:17 and the crowing, out of the tunnel, part of waking reality, was repeated with enthusiastic, vigorous, electrifying stridency. It took me a few moments to remember last night's scene: the endless struggle, the frenetic flapping of wings, the eyes that resisted, that refused to cloud over, my aching hands and wrists: the body fell lifeless to the ground; I threw it into a corner and covered it with earth; I remembered him as if I could still see him; I covered him with earth; he looked like a pile of dirty rags . . .

I dressed early and packed my suitcases. After 7:00 you could hear footsteps in the kitchen. That's where I went. The landlady, her back to the door, was preparing her husband's breakfast. I spoke rapidly, feeling that any interruption would be fatal:

"Señora, don't worry; I'm prepared to pay for the rooster. Unless he's still alive, he hasn't died; obviously, unless he's still in good health . . . but I don't think so. It must have been another one that crowed. Are there roosters in the neighborhood? And also please give me my bill. I'm leaving this morning."

She looked at me in silence, probably surprised but not showing any reaction. With great deliberation she cleaned her hands on a cloth and turned around. I was afraid then that she'd explode and try to scratch my eyes out.

"Sit down," she said, pointing to a chair next to the marble table. I obeyed.

"Wouldn't you like a little coffee?"

I thought of the small attention they offer condemned prisoners just a few minutes before they execute them. I was sitting in the hotseat and had no desire to drink coffee with the landlady—my longing to get away from the boardinghouse was turning into a compulsion—but there was no way to refuse. She passed me the sugar and then, something unheard of—she set out toast, honey, cake, a piece of sausage . . .

"Help yourself . . ."

I had a knot in the pit of my stomach, but I began to eat so as not to offend her. The food barely got down my throat.

"You know something?" the landlady began after a moment. "My husband can't stand that rooster either. He really is very annoying with all that noise at 5:00 in the morning . . ."

I felt the toast and honey and the coffee with milk go down easier. I was even tempted to take a bit of sausage.

"Well, it's a shame you're leaving," said the landlady.

"I'm going to my mother's house," I improvised. "The poor woman is suffering a good deal because she is alone."

"In that case," said the landlady, "you're doing the right thing. You have to be a good son."

I insisted on trying to pay her for the rooster, and she refused to hear any more about it. Pay her for what? I came to the conclusion that the rooster had been resurrected, that the crowing at dawn . . . But the inert body sticking to my hands damp with perspiration . . . ?

The landlady wished me lots of luck and hoped that my mother would be well. I asked permission to come back later to pick up my suitcases, and she told me of course, whenever I wanted.

Then I walked for over an hour, hoping the exercise would calm me down, and I ended up on the lower Alameda in a café I had never been to before. The feeling that your life is changing is always accompanied by a strange, irresistible pleasure, but it doesn't last long (I know this from experience). I watch them unloading a beer truck, a cart that goes wobbling by filled with vegetables, two nuns who are crossing the street, the new paint shining on an automobile, with the feeling that I am discovering the universe for the first time. Later, I know, habit destroys everything. And you decide that changing—houses, jobs, wives, friends—wasn't worth the effort. But your bridges have been burned; what else can you do? Experience is a hard teacher. Don't I know it!

Perhaps I'll go live with my mother. After all, she's seen that I'll leave like a shot if she starts in with her manias. Even she has to learn from experience. When all is said and done, if the two of us are living alone, the most logical, natural thing, one would say . . . If she starts in with her manias . . . I'll call her right from this café. It will make her very happy. I'm certain she must have learned her lesson. She won't start in with her manias. When all is said and done . . . The novelty doesn't last very long. Why change, when you get right down to it? . . . I remember the Argentinian graphologist, the one with the scapulary covering the hair on his chest. It was funny to see him jump into the water with the scapulary bobbing up and down right in the middle of all the foam and the splashing and the other bathers. He had a monkey face. He insisted on being alone with the one he was going to talk to; afterward we rushed up to the person to hear all about it.

This time his predictions are really not going to come true. When all is said and done, the most reasonable thing, if the two of us are living alone . . . No more changes! Back to the old life and live in peace . . . In fact, it's the only reasonable way. Even the landlady had to admit that. Incredible. I never would have believed it. Passing me toast with honey. And my hands still hurt from the struggle. How that bird resisted death! Everything in the universe resists death. It sounds like one of the Argentinian's phrases. I'll telephone now.

"Do you have slugs for the phone?"

Peralta, he's going to laugh when he finds out.

BEGIN AGAIN

A. POULIN, JR.

I
Like some migratory creature
    whose survival hinges on a yearly trek
        back to its species' native breeding grounds,

I have returned to this small coastal town
    in Maine where everything decays too soon
        and nothing ever dies quite soon enough.

Here, in the haze of oaks and elms ablaze
    with no more than a residue
        of oxygen and sap, cracked and peeling

plaster casts of dwarfed deer graze on blistered
    grass; whiter every day, winter brooding
        in their intricately beautiful and

brainless skulls, they inch toward old abandoned
    porches that will never be consoled,
        toward the char, the sudden frost, the utter

desolation at the heart of every
    open eye and palm. I was born here.
        My father's buried here, his father,

mother, and his brothers, all aligned
    precisely in the family plot according
        to the schema of our tree, and they root

themselves and me more deeply in this
    rocky ground than when we tried to work
        it for a living. Tonight I sit alone

absorbing darkness resonating with
    the ancient music of the sea, the echo
        of our common tomb, while far above that

distant, bare Atlantic field the faces
    of my family bloom, a brilliant tribal
        constellation ruling in a starless sky.

II
My wife and daughter are asleep, their bodies
    glowing with the sunlight they've absorbed all
        day, refracting their excess of light back

into the dark that barely touches them.
    Each day these two women grow into more
        beautiful reflections of each other,

as their limbs enclose the day's last rays
    of sun like petals of dark flowers that are
        still strangers in this motherland of memory.

I walk into the light of their deep sleep
    and breathe the nimbus of their dream:
        let these lovely women sleep; let them wake

refreshed; let them slowly stretch themselves
    open to the sun again, dawn clinging
        to their bodies' down like brilliant dew;

and let them never get attached enough
    to this coastal land too long to live here
        as wild columbines flowering among the rocks.

Their history is unfolding in another
    land, a far more gentle future place
        where I may join them when my work is done.

Alone again, I inhale the dark
    like an ancient lover's breath: at last,
        tonight, brittle seeds of light begin

to orbit in my ankles, in my wrists,
    sail the unchartered inner space of bones,
        blossom with a meteoric fury in my mouth.

III
Like flocks of gulls around a fishing boat
    when the men are cleaning the day's catch,
        dumping heads and innards overboard, blood

blooming in the heaving sea like petals
    of ferocious underwater flowers,
        or as if my name were intricately etched

across the prism at the center of
    each atom constituting their genetic
        molecules, tonight again moths swarm out-

side my window, perch on the precise geo-
    metric interlacing of the screen
        gleaming like a membrane separating

need from mere ambition, a film between
    blank memory, the future's incandescence.
        You know the myth of moths among the folk

here: they say they're souls of dead lovers,
    relatives and friends granted a reprieve
        from darkness one night every year to hunt

the living, offer you the secrets
    of the dead imprinted on their wings,
        flashing in their desperate eyes, in exchange

for particles of light swimming in your
    blood—glimpses of a future where the memory
        of sons is the father's fullness of desire.

And if you can decipher that rare
    code, they will hunt you down again next year.
        This is my fortieth year. Those light-thirsty

angels have fished my veins a decade.
    I know more about the dead than any-
        body dies to know. The spoors of their

secrets root like mushrooms in
    the dank cellars of my chest where darkness
        rules and has been reigning far too long.

Knowing what was sown, what little ever
    flourished, what the fruit of that ambitious
        future surely is, finally the time

has come to cut myself off from a tree
    I never planted, to uproot myself
        from this unyielding land, to strip away

dead branches with those old nests and cocoons
    abandoned long ago, to set all that
        debris ablaze and to begin again.

IV
The lamp erects a fence and stakes out
    a small pasture of pure light on the edge
        of one more day that would collapse beneath

the weight of so much darkness at its
    center. Wild with the very smell of light,
        a galaxy of moths, their tiny faces as

familiar as mirrors, wings as delicate
    and decorated as tiny heirloom doilies
        embroidered by a tribe of lonely women,

gather like a herd of famished deer,
    after weeks of bitter winter, come
        to graze the orchard of my palm, gardens

of my two bare wrists. One by one I let
    them in, hold them in my outstretched hand
        with a cautious tenderness reserved

for the very fragile, the most precious
    of exotic flowers; one by one I speak
        their names with love, as it were my own:

Alfred, Alphonse, Melanie, Aurora,
    Azarie, Rose, Napoleon, Ovila, Emile,
        Florida, Evangeline, William, Laurier . . .

and one by one, in a measure of more
    light than they have ever known, without
        any compromise, for a moment that will

last them an eternity, they breathe,
    they rise, they suddenly disintegrate
        in the acetylene of my loving breath.

V
My table's littered with small stars of ash,
>a burnt-out nebula that would never
>>fill the cupped hand of my sleeping daughter.

Before dawn breaks above the bay, before
>my wife and daughter wake, never knowing
>>that the constellation of those ruling

planets rooted in the vast Atlantic sky
>vanished as they slept, with my night's
>>work done, like a factory hand after one

more eight-hour shift, I wash the oil
>and soot clinging to my hands and face and
>>stretch out in the glowing garden of our bed.

Dawn: a full and brilliant orange sun
>rises from the sea, slowly hauling sound-
>>less echoes of itself from deep within

our lungs, reverberating in our
>open mouths and leaping from our lips,
>>as bright sonatas bloom inside our brains.

FIVE POEMS

MARY JANE WHITE

TOILETTE DE VIOLETTE

I, Leduc, splash attar of roses
over my poor, huge, runny nose,

red from my summer cold. No, wretchedness.
Crying and crying-in-the-mirror. Why!

why do I feel such tenderness?
For whom? If I turn away, there is no one

really, either. I see a near horizon, the sun,
small, sweet cockade of a window's lock,

and purple spread through the sky like a woman's
eyelid closing down—so. Inside my head

are green and yellow blobs, a paperweight
or loyal animal. If I could make a human face

appear! A stranger passed our café on Friday.

His heart chirped, *little chap,* like the wicked fellow
that it was, and patted me through my new raincoat—

thump-*thump,* thump-*thump,* and bought itself an absinthe.
Why did we ever want to be sexual in our companionship?

Sitting forward to write this, I twist a fingerful
of stringy hair, yours, mine,

trying to make us prettier, Gabriel.

LINDEMAN

Your last name's the one I remember. Director
of our all-American chorus, you led me alone

into the sandhills, told me how you were named
for the lindens that grow like smaller oaks
or elms in Europe's parks, and which, translated

into English are "lime trees" usually.
You were smaller too. Your head and profile
should have crowned a height of six or seven feet.

Lindeman is spicy now I've smelled a linden blooming
and been reminded a time or two of you
kissing me, first of anyone. A *lime* has always been

a green lemon to my mind, but I thought you yellower then,
with age. Now so many have kissed me too.
Still, of them all, you were my good instructor,

the single, high-placed person I hoped to hold
as you would open your arms in preparation for a note
to break from, as I would guess, two hundred girls.

I was your girl, that one day only, at the beach,
where you noticed me out of six or seven. We'd worked

to bury you, helpless to the neck. Dark glasses.
That left your voice and even teeth. Deep breath.
Sand broke off your chest. Alarming. Now I would rhyme

with my early thinking, call it *charming*.
Then we walked, not far, and sat without a towel.

No waves, no stars, no air to gasp to start with.
Your hand ran under my suit-strap and let it snap.
I thought probably I would hate you, but I have not.

WALKING ON A FIELD

I look in one direction
at a time. Peripheral vision's there,
but blurred in coming
to me by a small
infirmity I can't

expect to conquer once like
virginity or a mountaintop.
It's something I do
try to compensate
for—turning my head, whole

body to see. I feel a
little awkward and that is all as
I watch my friend's brisk
approach. We walk off
together; a cornstalk

turns on its pithy axis
as we come up, pass by its twirled blade-
like leaves, bent tassel
and swathed, full cob dropped
like the forefoot of a

bee, all golden-bleached. I draw
you one, but a good number—thousands
of these—remotely
like ourselves—stand
rustling intimately

in their ordered rows, each in
wry, minimal contact. Rooted, how
can they help but move
as they do, and bow
to hail, sleet, wind, and snow,

finally. Still, to speak of
these too sadly's to step ahead of
ourselves—up rises
the present, gentle,
mounded hill, plowed and

easily taken for
a pastoral *but* to Iowa's
flatness. The story
about that hill is:
a tractor flipped over

on a farmer and killed him
bloodily. This field's his place and his
absence—not so much
to us as to the
several people in his

house. Sad homily, sad old
earth's story, it's hard and right we see
enough to know a bit
about him, to make
a forcible entry.

SOUTH BEAR

You come up behind me,
a new man,
having caught, finally,
a fish, you confess,
with only the dip-net.
Explain as you will,
the skill involved,
your integrity at first,
casting for hours,
I can see you knee-deep
in icy running water.
I have seen you,
swooping so hard
you were liable to fall
backwards, stomping
up the stream bottom,
chubs and trout
swimming like crazy
before your eyes.
What's the risk
of a fine
that would break us
for months?
All told, it's
a valuable fish
we have here—
something to eat,
something to picture,
a piece of the rainbow
to argue over—
its right length,
the date,
what sort of
bait to recommend
to Chris, a novice
and friend.

WANTING A BRIGHT BABY

I laid John Donne, spine up,
flat over my chart of menstrual cycles,
a one night's marriage of science and art
and artless hope. If I'm ever two
that will be more than you could do, John Donne,
or a woman alone.
I reach back for you. Alive
as I am, I'll never have the pleasure of your offer.
I'd not refuse you, or be true
overlong, if flesh would resurrect
your bones and love move you again and your soul
come back and your mind
descend.
      You could go as low
as me, I think, and did,
happily and quick.
Still I hope if I could have you
I would make you slow to overrun
and deeply sweet, as all good fun.

LA VITA NUOVA

GEOFFREY RIPS

The messenger arrives before the message arrives. "Sometimes that happens," he explains. He stands there puffing at the top of the stairs, looking wistfully back down behind him.

Ah, Beatrice! To know you is not to know you in a thousand ways. I first saw Beatrice coming on to Sanso in MacDonald's. She stroked the edge of her fish sandwich, laughing too loudly at all his stupid Uruguayan jokes. How does a Paraguayan screw in the bulb?

The next time was across the subway platform. The doors of the subway opened. A man in a blue conductor's uniform went hurtling onto the train, hit his head against the doors of the opposite side, and fell to the floor. The doors closed, and there was Beatrice inside, her face pressed against the window of the car, her palms pressed against her ears as a signal indicating terror. But she was express, and she was gone.

That was always the way with her. Beatrice—not a window, not a door between us. Too close to be the world and too close not to be. A blur in the middle distance, when all the rest is clearly seen. Unescapable legs. Inevitable Beatrice. A change of earth. A change of air. You go to the grocery, and the waters part. Pay the newsboy, and the trees lose their leaves.

Her twenty-four hours were my twelve. Her twelve were my seven days. Even in bed. She is wrapped around me before I know it. And before I know it she is gone. Or it is the middle of the night, and she is on me, waking me and telling me to sleep, crying that she is far

171

ahead of me or that she has fallen behind and wait, I must wait for her to catch up. Oh Beatrice.

Or that night we find ourselves sitting across from a man wearing an electric tie. Red and yellow lines swim into his chin. He pretends the tie is not electric. He reads the newspaper while fingering the cleft in his chin. But you are not fooled. You point to the plug taped to his ankle, to the extension cord running out the bottom of his left pants leg. We are glad we chose this subway car.

In the one ahead of us a man sits with his head completely bandaged. As the train pulled in, we heard him moan. In the one behind, another man nods his head in sleep, his tongue licking the railing.

Ah Beatrice, they are trying to move us out and away from each other. Today they arrived at seven and took the chairs. Yesterday the lamp. What are we to do? The gap between the subway cars looms larger.

We inch through a tunnel. Smoke drifts in through the windows. A small girl sitting on a suitcase puts her head on your knees. You finally tell me about Teo. How he rearranged the letters of your name. Trecibea Cebarite Atreibec. How he dropped some letters when he felt like it and added others. Trice Tric Beat Bete Ma Bete. How he sent you application forms lifted from the registration desks of colleges, ripped from cereal boxes, torn from plumbing supply displays. Humiliation upon humiliation. How one night he killed the azaleas, biting off the flowers one by one and spitting the petals on your mouth, your hair, your breasts, your eyes. How you let him. How he would not stop. How you would not make him stop. Oh Beatrice. A blind man stands up and furiously rubs his eye sockets with his fists. Take that. And that. Beatrice, ma bête, shall I jump between the cars?

The last time I saw you was on the ferry to Staten Island. How many times did we make that trip, the air so deadly and still in all the listless shafts of Manhattan? Each time you couldn't wait, beating on the huge iron doors of the terminal, Jeanne d'Arc for all the people sitting on the long green wooden benches in the middle of the night. And the bell would finally ring. And the doors would finally swing open, and Beatrice would raise her arm for me to follow and for them to follow. And I followed, but they just stayed there as the doors closed on their long green rows.

And we were out on the deck, on the bottom deck with the metal floor and the cars. You wanted the spray in your face. You gripped the side of the ferry and rode the deck like a circus performer, plunging into the waves, defying the timbers of the launching slip, saluting the liberty statue. Is history the adoration of false progress? you once asked there. The annihilation of nostalgia? Is it the diminishing resonance of despair? Who cares? The ghost freighters stand in the water in the night. The glister of refineries and back to Manhattan's steaming wall thrown up against the cool winds from the west and the ocean.

Some nights back and forth across the water several times. The top deck, the front, the back, the bottom, but never inside. Even in the rain. We watched lightning move across in front of us, meet us just above Liberty Island, explode in our faces, charging the spray. Until the last time, when the man beside you wearing only shorts and hiking boots asked you for a cigarette, and when you turned to ask me he slipped over the rail and into the sound of the waters. You turned back, and he was not there. But another man was there looking out into the waves, his mouth open as if to scream. Then more men and women. Then one threw a life preserver. Then many threw. And the ferry engines cut off. The horn for alarm was sounded. They played searchlights across the indifferent bay. More people came forward. You held your arms across your stomach and stepped back against a wall. We stayed there in the water, surrounded by bobbing life preservers, you pressed against the wall. Then some of the preservers were cut loose and others pulled in. We continued to the slip at Staten Island. When the landing platform came down, you were, as always, the first to board the arching plank, to feel your weight slowly bring its back to level. The platform came down, and you walked away.

Oh Beatrice. The leaves on the tree outside my window are turning red one at a time. On a field, viridian, a leaf stem, gules.

The messenger turns his face away. He puffs and heaves. He throws up his fat and inky hands. "I don't know what to say," he says. He hangs his head. He walks back down the stairs.

SEVEN POEMS

NICHOLAS BORN

Translated from the German by Agnes Stein

1 OVER THE MOUNTAINS

Between victory and peace
storms have been driven into corners.
We see this clearly and give
our yeas.
I and you one heart and one soul
search for each other on hills in the first snow
on the rough growth of high plains
on Winterberg.
You call hallo into the Ebbe Mountains
I call hallo into the Lenne Valley.
At one time all was different.
Foxes are lonely in the winter
we too part and freeze
so that we can write:
Rain day after day
today an early sunset, one sits
between walls and leads a heavy life.
No motion in the room, everywhere
the doll lies about
the red blue yellow knit

by my niece you know her, Iris.
One must be less demanding but
nothing surpasses something special.
Woods Sauerland you know are
rather nice without rain. But it
grows dark early now I must close: let us
not lose touch.

2 GOOD-BYE

Who will paint me a picture of my friends
in a collapsible frame convenient for pockets
I am going away
leaving behind a doubtful hole
in these tightly knit rows

Friends you have taught me to fear
with you and with beer it is wrong to age
teeth will fall out in the community
in the most comfortable of all collectives

Be good to your women, be better than me
I will take over a wobbling smoking section
go friends into self-righteousness
the weather remains changeable
may you badly come off badly

Good-bye have I forgotten anything
return everything that belongs to me
yes I am growing mean fellows

3 THE UNMASKING EYE

And when so many worlds are forgotten
Who are the great forgetters
Who is it that keeps parts of worlds from us
Who is the Columbus whose fault it is
that a continent disappears
(after Apollinaire)

4 IN THE D-TRAIN MUNICH–HANOVER

Heads are rolling in railway stations
gloomy September 77
hillside vines tumble into color
on the barrows the boxes hold time fuses.
Small boats on the Main.
The light is peaceful
peaceful the smoker on the canal
on the lawn new faces with the ball.

5
DIFFICULTIES are on the increase:
what seems comprehensible today
reverses itself.
It is difficult
while walking to order thoughts when
trains cross our paths
to locate oneself on a city map
with disturbing airplanes overhead.

It is difficult
to remain in the outer suburbs
where every movement has room
with ambiguous movement for despair—
difficult at the same time to take note
when the sun breaks through clouds
a cafe opens or
in the winter when in the snowy park
a lady's shoe finds
a hard-packed track leading straight
to one's own door.
There one stands and bares
teeth to oneself alone.
When the lips close again
brother and sister are dead.

6
OVER THE HOUSES a weather vane rises—
misery is not complete.
Life is fun
so long it has enemies
life goes on so long
it profits.
The seamless sky this fall
rises above the harvest. Stubbornly
peace progresses.
No one is surprised any longer.
Death to be comprehended must
be divided by its mass. Numbers
are a musical factor, generate
popular opinion.
The quick retort does not serve us
we much prefer a whine.

7 THREE WISHES

Aren't facts annoying and boring?
Wouldn't it be better to have three wishes
with the condition they all be fulfilled?
I wish for a life without long pauses
wherein walls are being searched for projectiles
a life whose leaves are not torn off
    by cashiers.
I wish to write letters which
    contain me wholly.
I wish for a book in which you all enter in the front
    and come out in the back.
And I would like not to forget that it's nicer
to love you than not to love you.

A YELLOW RABBIT FULL OF HELIUM

Fourteen Tankas

ANDRÉ LEFEVERE

Summer—old people
in the bars around the square
watching their faces
on both sides of the windows
in the slow evening drizzle.

A thin old lady
on her way to hospital
a suitcase to keep
death at bay and a pair of
new shoes in a plastic bag.

A small town churchyard
all the headstones arranged in
strict chronology
the gravedigger parks his Datsun
between two generations.

A small butterfly
in the Greyhound terminal
unfolding its wings
on a crumpled newspaper:
your free color supplement.

A fat gentleman
in breeches, ruffles and lace
staring at the floor
exhibit 4/28
"The Revolutionary."

He sees her getting
out of a bus in New York
calls her name and runs
after her; she just walks on,
six hours ahead of him.

Father and daughter
jogging on the beach at night
same T shirts, same shorts
same smile, same sneakers, their breasts
swaying to the same rhythm.

Children trying out
the latest game on the streets
of San Salvador:
one gets blindfolded, the rest
take a few steps back and shoot.

From the balcony
he sees a yellow rabbit
full of helium

floating by on a mattress
of wind in the noonday sun.

The old translator
insists that his guest drink up
the last of the wine
that way he's sure to come back
says the proverb, but not when.

The poet has moved
to his new house by the sea;
after a few walks
on the beach he starts calling
all the gulls by their first names.

The light is still red
when she starts crossing the street
in her see-through blouse
the cars come to heel, growling
at her lacquered toes, bright green.

Haydn's Creation,
flute and soprano flirting
a discreet duet
under the disapproving
gaze of the full orchestra.

A little girl makes
tea: she pours a big kettle
of boiling nothing
into a plastic teapot
and lets it steep for ever.

NOTES ON CONTRIBUTORS

DIERDRA BALDWIN's long experimental poem, *The Emerging Detail* (The Word Works, 1978), was a finalist for the William Carlos Williams Prize and has also appeared in a Spanish translation. Other publications include *An Occasional Suite*, which appeared both as a book (Jazz Press) and a performance tape (Watershed Foundation) in 1981, *Inside Outside* (1982), and a small volume, tentatively titled *Totomic*, to be brought out by Burning Deck Press in 1983.

CAROL JANE BANGS directs literature programs for the Centrum Foundation in Port Townsend, Washington. A chapbook, *Irreconcilable Differences*, was published in Lewiston, Idaho, in 1978.

MACLIN BOCOCK's work has appeared in such quarterlies as *Fiction International*, *The Southern Review*, *Canto*, and *The Denver Quarterly*.

The late West German writer NICHOLAS BORN (1934–79) is probably best known in this country for his novel *The Deception* (Little, Brown, 1983), which was the basis for Volcker Schlöndorff's film *Circle of Deceit*. Born, however, was honored as a poet with the German Petrarc and Rilke prizes, a fellowship in Rome, and a guest lectureship at the University of Iowa. AGNES STEIN has published original poetry and translations in England and the U.S. She is editor-translator of *Four German Poets: Eich, Domin, Fried, and Kunert* (1980) and of *Windy Times: The Selected Works of Günter Kunert* (1983), both published by Red Dust.

New Directions publishes ERNESTO CARDENAL's *In Cuba* (1974), *Apocalypse and Other Poems* (1977), and *Zero Hour and Other Documentary Poems* (1980). Father Cardenal, a Marxist and a priest, is presently Nicaragua's Minister of Culture. JONATHAN COHEN's translations appear in *Zero Hour* and also in Enrique Lihn's *The Dark Room and Other Poems* (New Directions, 1978). In 1981, he was awarded a grant from the National Endowment for the Arts to translate Cardenal's early poems, including the two which appear in these pages.

A professor of writing at Texas Technical University, DOUG CROWELL's work has appeared in *ND40* and *Mississippi Review*. He has received a National Endowment for the Arts grant for a novel in progress.

The poet and newspaper publisher PABLO ANTONIO CUADRA is well known in his native Nicaragua. Translations of fourteen of his poems appear in the translations section of *The Collected Poems* of Thomas Merton (New Directions, 1977). *Seven Trees against the Dying of the Light*, from which the poems appearing here are taken, was composed during Somoza's last years, 1977-79. STEVEN WHITE is a translator who makes his home in Eugene, Oregon.

PHILIPPE DENIS studied at the Sorbonne with Roland Barthes and Gaeten Picon, receiving his degree in 1973. The first of his three collections, *Cahier d'ombres*, won the celebrated Cino del Duca Prize and was illustrated in a special edition by Joan Miro before being published in 1974 by Mercure de France. This was followed by *Revif* (Maeght, 1978), and *Carnet d'un aveuglement* (Flammarion, 1980). Denis has received grants from the Centre National des Lettres and a Fulbright for teaching literature at the University of Minnesota. He has also translated into French the poems of Emily Dickinson, Marianne Moore, and Sylvia Plath. MARK IRWIN, a professor of English at Case Western Reserve University, is the translator of Philippe Denis's *Notebook of Shadows: Selected Poems 1974–1980* (Globe Press, 1982).

JOSEPH DONAHUE is currently working toward his Ph.D. in English at Columbia University, where he received an M.F.A. in 1979.

In spite of being sent to Cuba by the Allende government, the Chilean writer, editor, and diplomat JORGE EDWARDS was expelled from there by Fidel Castro. Edwards then joined Pablo Neruda at the Chilean embassy in Paris, where he remained until the present junta came to power and expelled him from the diplomatic service. He has published the autobiographical *Persona Non Grata* and a novel, *El Museo de Cera*. EDITH GROSSMAN is the author of *The Antipoetry of Nicanor Parra* (New York University Press, 1975). Her translations of poetry and prose from the Spanish have appeared widely.

184 NOTES ON CONTRIBUTORS

PETER GLASSGOLD's Old English translations of poems by Ezra Pound and William Carlos Williams have appeared in *Modern Poetry in Translation 1983* (Persea Books). Rumors that he is reconstructing a three-thousand-line epic palindrome from the Provençal are exaggerated. The language in question is simply Norman French.

Kentucky born, New York bred, and a graduate of Harvard, J. B. GOODENOUGH lives with her husband and children in a small Massachusetts town. Her poems have appeared in numerous journals.

Through his writings on mathematics, sociology, history, philosophy, and literature, LARS GUSTAFSSON's influence has been strong in all quarters of the European academic community. In his native Sweden, he has published in virtually every area of *belles lettres*. New Directions has brought out two of his novels: *The Death of a Beekeeper* (1981), and *The Tennis Players* (1983). YVONNE SANDSTROEM, a professor of English at Southern Massachusetts University, rendered *The Tennis Players* into English. Her translation of one of Gustafsson's poems has appeared in *The New Yorker*.

RUSSELL HALEY, whose work also appeared in *ND42* and *ND43*, lives in New Zealand, where his first collection of stories, *The Sauna Bath Mysteries*, came out in 1978. Earlier publications, of poetry, were *The Walled Garden* (1972) and *On the Fault Line* (1977). *Northern Lights*, an extended but discontinuous narrative, is in progress.

WILLIAM HOLINGER is a junior fellow at the Michigan Society of Fellows and an assistant professor in the Department of English at the University of Michigan, where he teaches creative writing. His fiction has appeared in the *Western Humanities Review, North American Review, Canto,* and previous New Directions Anthologies.

Belgian-born ANDRÉ LEFEVERE teaches literature at the University of Antwerp. He has translated widely into English from the French, Greek, Dutch, and German, and his translation, with Michael Hamburger, of Philippe Jacottet's *Seedtime* was published by New Directions in 1977. His own poetry and prose have also appeared in *ND30* and *ND34*.

In 1983, New Directions is bringing out DENISE LEVERTOV's *Poems 1960–1967*. *Light Up the Cave* (prose) was published in 1981 and a collection of new poetry, *Candles in Babylon*, in 1982.

One of Brazil's major literary figures, the late CLARICE LISPECTOR wrote numerous novels and short story collections, which have been translated into French, German, Spanish, Italian and Czech. In this country, Knopf published her novel *The Apple in the Dark*, and her short story collection, *Family Ties*, was brought out by the University of Texas press. ALEXIS LEVITIN's translations of Lispector's short stories appear in New American Library's *Latin American Literature Today* (1977). His translations of Lispector and other writers have been published in numerous periodicals, including *Translation, Fiction*, and *Mother Jones*.

MICHAEL MCGUIRE's plays have been produced in San Francisco, Los Angeles, and points between, as well as abroad. His plays and stories have appeared in *Paris Review* and *The Hudson Review*, and he has lectured on drama and creative writing at universities in the U.S., Canada, and Saudi Arabia. Apart from a recent two-month stay at Yaddo, he has been living in Oregon for many years.

The author of *The Autobiography of Cassandra: Princess and Prophetess of Troy* (Archer Editions, 1979), *Bastards: Footnotes to History* (Treacle, 1979), and *Encores for a Dilettante* (Fiction Collective, 1978), URSULE MOLINARO lives in New York City. Her work also appeared in *ND43*.

ROBERT NICHOLS is the author of a tetralogy, *Daily Lives in Nghsi-Altai*, published by New Directions between 1977 and 1979.

For information on "Seven New Zealand Poets," see the notes following the selections.

A. POULIN, JR., is a poet, anthologist, and translator, and the editor of BOA Editions. He has recently completed a translation of Rainer Maria Rilke's four hundred French poems, for which he was awarded a translator's grant from the National Endowment for the Arts, and he is now working on an anthology of Quebecois poetry in translation. "Begin Again" is the title poem from his new collection of poems.

ALEKSIS RANNIT, one of the foremost poets in the Estonian language, is curator of Russian and East European Studies at the Library of Yale University. His work has appeared frequently in these pages.

A former co-ordinator of the Freedom to Write program of PEN American Center, GEOFFREY RIPS has returned to his native Texas, where he edits *The Texas Observer*. His *Unamerican Activities: The Campaign Against the Underground Press in the United States 1960–1979* was brought out by City Lights Books in 1981.

MARY JANE WHITE practices law in Decorah, Iowa.

New Directions will publish *Clothes for a Summer Hotel*, a recent play by TENNESSEE WILLIAMS, in 1983.